GROWING UP METRIC

"I, like George, read a lot of business books. I don't have time for the bad ones, but I am totally absorbed by the good ones. This is a book about personal and business growth, and not only did I like it, but I want my children to read it. George is an energetic enthusiast. He is passionate about what he likes and always wants to learn more. And he has poured his wisdom into this book. He has an easy writing style, and you will feel he is talking to you personally, sharing what he knows from his own business and his personal experiences, with a sprinkle of valuable philosophy. He extracts nuggets of practical advice from all that experience and shares them tactfully. This book is about people, life, reality, vision, and balance that you will love—even if you are not building a business."

—*Michael De Clercq, president, TransContinental Trade & Finance Corp.*

"A healthy batch of business awesomeness from a CEO who knows his way around success."

—*Dan Waldschmidt, extreme athlete and best-selling author*

"Reading *Growing Up Metric* is like sitting down with an old friend and a bottle of wine as he reflects on what has and what hasn't worked over a long, interesting, and successful career running his family business. In this real-life 'parable,' which is equal parts personal path and business journey, George intertwines the best ideas from dozens of great business and personal productivity leaders with his own pearls of wisdom in a way that makes each idea that much more understandable and actionable. I'd recommend pairing *Growing Up Metric* with a good Pinot Noir."

—*John Verry, CEO, Pivot Point Security*

"This book has succinctly demonstrated simple techniques and real-life suggestions that have not only worked for the author but have some of the foundations that have brought our company to where we are today. This quick read re-invigorated me to improve upon my leadership role as CEO and to fight the fear to delegate the things that others can do to not only free up my own time but to empower the leaders around me."

—*Noah Baskin, CEO, Tower Water*

"If you've ever dreamed of having your own business, or if you've ever wondered how to take your business to the next level, this book is for you. George shares his lifetime of business lessons in a frank, transparent way that is certain to enrich you and your business. Instead of learning the hard way through trial and error, I suggest you read this book and take years off your learning curve. I loved George's real-life stories and his easy-to-apply insights, and you will too."

—*Dr. Alan Zimmerman, author of* The Payoff Principle: Discover the
3 Secrets for Getting What You Want out of Life and Work

"Far too many business leaders fail to recognize and capitalize on the importance of building and sustaining relationships, reputations, trust, and confidence from their prospects, partners, and the market in general. This book nails it. It very well may be the competitive differentiator you need to make and exceed your number this year."

—*Matt Heinz, president, Heinz Marketing, Inc.*

"George Contos offers you a window into the mind-set of a second-generation captain who continues to beat the odds (only 30 percent of family businesses make it to the second generation). For multigenerational companies, he amplifies the imperative for family awareness, difficult conversations, and clear agreements. His leadership thrives on a passion for constant learning and a positive approach. The result has been consistent annual growth for World Wide Metric since 2000. I have worked with family business owners for over fourteen years. George truly represents the success so many entrepreneurs seek today. His voice speaks to us from pragmatic know-how and 'been there, done that' experience (both positive and negative). This is a great read for any entrepreneur navigating the difficult transitions of growth, family ownership, and leadership."

—*David Paul Carter, principal, David Paul Carter Consulting, LLC*

"*Growing Up Metric* delivers a wealth of real-world knowledge that can benefit anyone from the up-and-coming entrepreneur to the seasoned executive. It contains a treasure trove of actionable advice—with an emphasis on helping you master the basics required for climbing the ladder of success."

—*Rob Colasanti, director of admissions, The Abraham Group*

"In the eight-plus years I've known George Contos, he has been a continual source of inspiration and ideas for me. His dynamic approach to business, as well as sales, is very evident in this book, and the World Wide Metric story is a great case study in building a company of best practices and a culture of excellence."

—*Tracy J. Martin, president, Martin Insurance Group*

It's rare when a business finds and stays focused on a niche that 10x's the company. World Wide Metric has done it and shares their practical secrets any firm can follow.

—*Verne Harnish, author of Scaling Up*

"The stories and lessons in Growing Up Metric will inspire new leaders and help guide them through the landmines of business."

—*Darren Hardy, CEO mentor, New York Times bestselling author, and publisher/editor of SUCCESS magazine*

GROWING UP
METRIC

GROWING UP
METRIC

REAL-LIFE BUSINESS INSIGHTS
for REALIZING YOUR POTENTIAL

GEORGE CONTOS

Published by Advantage, Charleston, South Carolina.
Member of Advantage Media Group.

ADVANTAGE is a registered trademark, and the Advantage colophon is a trademark of Advantage Media Group, Inc.

Printed in the United States of America.

ISBN: 978-1-59932-638-2
LCCN: 2016938616

Book design by Matthew Morse.

This publication is designed to provide accurate and authoritative information in regard to the subject matter covered. It is sold with the understanding that the publisher is not engaged in rendering legal, accounting, or other professional services. If legal advice or other expert assistance is required, the services of a competent professional person should be sought.

Advantage Media Group is proud to be a part of the Tree Neutral® program. Tree Neutral offsets the number of trees consumed in the production and printing of this book by taking proactive steps such as planting trees in direct proportion to the number of trees used to print books. To learn more about Tree Neutral, please visit **www.treeneutral.com.** To learn more about Advantage's commitment to being a responsible steward of the environment, please visit **www.advantagefamily.com/green**

Advantage Media Group is a publisher of business, self-improvement, and professional development books and online learning. We help entrepreneurs, business leaders, and professionals share their Stories, Passion, and Knowledge to help others Learn & Grow. Do you have a manuscript or book idea that you would like us to consider for publishing? Please visit **advantagefamily.com** or call **1.866.775.1696.**

I would like to dedicate this book to my three children,
Alessandra, Rylan, and Natalia.

Don't ever give up on your dreams!
Live life! Don't let life live you.

TABLE OF CONTENTS

ACKNOWLEDGMENTS

There are so many people I would like to acknowledge and thank for having been influences in my life. They helped shape me as a man and businessman and now as an author. There are many books that I have read, devoured, and scribbled in, and many of the authors of those books have become my mentors. Here is the short list: Earl Nightingale, Dale Carnegie, Napoleon Hill, Ralph Waldo Emerson, Jim Collins, Jay Abraham, Verne Harnish, Darren Hardy, Tony Robbins, Brian Tracy, Brendon Burchard, Harry Dent, Seth Godin, Patrick Lencioni, Malcolm Gladwell, Simon Sinek, and so many more. Thanks for inspiring and teaching me with your words and passion.

Thanks to Jay and Marilyn Westrom at Dale Carnegie Training for giving me the opportunity to strut my stuff.

To my dear friend and colleague of my entire career, Maria Soler. You have been like a big sister, friend, and confidant like no other. Thanks for standing by my side all these years.

A huge thanks to my mom and dad, who have been among the greatest influences of my life and had to put up with a whole lot of crap from me, so I could grow up and be the man I am today. Thank you for teaching me the patience and humility that every leader needs.

Thanks to my brother and sister (and business partners), Theo and Anthee Contos. None of this would have been possible without your support and loyalty in blindly following my pursuits, beliefs, and dreams to all corners. This is as much yours as it is mine.

None of this could have happened without the tireless work of my editor, Jenny Tripp, and all the people at Advantage who helped me take a twenty-year-old dream and make it a reality. Thank you.

To my marketing team, Kate, Marissa, and Michael—thank you for your editorial notes to help hone the message of this book. You made my work on this project so much easier.

To my children, Alessandra, Rylan, and Natalia: you guys inspire me every day to go out into the world and do my very best. Thanks for supporting all my travels, despite the few missed meals and bed times they caused.

Last, but not least, to my dear wife Jessica, who besides being the best mom in the world, is also the best partner in the world. They say behind every great man is a great woman; well, I am proud to say that you are my wife, and your holding me to a higher standard is something every good man deserves to have. Thanks for believing in me and bringing out the best in me. I would not have wanted to do any of this without you.

INTRODUCTION

You're living the dream as a business owner, so why does it so often feel like a nightmare?

Whether you are a second-generation family business owner who has risen through the ranks to lead the company or a new owner who has purchased a business from its founder to move it to the next level, it's likely that you're working too hard and accomplishing too little. No matter how hard you push, it feels as though you're stuck in neutral. There are processes, procedures, and a whole company mind-set in place that do not align with you or your values; you know that you have to put *your* stamp on the company and get your team behind you, but you're not sure how.

No one ever said that running a company was easy. You cannot assume anything, and you cannot take things for granted, but you can learn—and learn and adapt you must. They say that if you love what you do, you never work a day in your life. There is some truth to that statement, and there is also the reality that running a company is hard work. It can be unrewarding, dreadfully boring, and even painful. Such is the life of a leader. But leading a business can also be the most rewarding thing you have ever done—something that brings you great joy and fulfillment.

I took over as CEO of the family company in 2000, when it was a $3.5 million business. After taking the helm, my brother, my sister, and I began changing some of the ways in which things had always been done and setting a new course for the company. By 2015, we had grown the company to $18 million in sales, and we currently have our sights on $25 million and $50 million within ten years. Yes, these are some big goals, but as they say, it's better to shoot for the stars and miss than to aim at the ground and hit. We now have over fifty employees in five locations, and further plans of expansion are in the works. These positive changes are a result of our hard work, collaboration, and good fortune.

My brother, my sister, and I are extremely fortunate to work with a very dedicated and determined team of people who have helped cultivate this work environment we call our home away from home. The concepts you'll find in this book have been tested and proven by action; they are not just theory. I hope that what I share with you here helps you on your path to building a business culture that works for you.

A BRIEF HISTORY OF OUR COMPANY

My father started his first company, World Wide Ship Repair, in Brooklyn, New York, in 1970. As he built his business, he saw the stateside need for metric standard products, such as valves and flanges, to conform to the international standards utilized by shipping companies in Europe and Asia.

By 1985, my dad sold the assets of the repair facility and went full blast into distribution, and World Wide Metric was born. My dad was and still is a hard-working man—relentless and tireless. He wanted to create a business he could pass along and that would take care of his family. Today, World Wide Metric remains a pipe, valve, and fitting supplier, specializing in metric components. We serve marine and industrial markets throughout North America and export our products around the world. By serving our clients with knowledgeable, friendly expertise, large inventories, on-time deliveries, and the fastest response time in the industry, we are an integral part of their supply chains.

THE ESSENTIALS FOR BUSINESS SUCCESS

Whether you're a budding entrepreneur or a second-generation owner, you will learn that there are four key impact areas every business owner needs to develop: (1) communication, (2) sales, (3) cash flow, and (4) marketing.

The first key area is communication—with employees, customers, vendors, and (most importantly) your family. Many times we become so focused on the business that we don't communicate well with family.

The second key area is the knowledge of how to build a sales team because sales drive revenue and growth. In sales and the pursuit of success at any level, you have to be relentless. I believe that everybody can be good at selling. We're all born salespeople. Whatever we want as a child, we instinctively know to relentlessly whine about it or repeat, "Can I have it? Can I have it? Can I have it?" a thousand times until our parents give in. Skill in sales is inherent in all of us—we just need to believe it and channel it. As the saying goes, nothing happens until someone sells something.

The third important skill that all entrepreneurs or business owners need is the ability to handle their cash flow. Cash flow is the oxygen of every business. Without it, companies can't grow sustainably and will wind up in debt. Payment collection is a hugely important aspect of every business—especially when you're taking one over.

The fourth key thing is marketing because no one else is going to market your business for you. *You* need to tell your story.

Time and time again, when I speak with leaders of struggling businesses, they are weak in one of these four areas. Ironically, they're weak in the one area that they're most concerned about but are also putting the least effort into. In this book, I'll dive into the challenges common to leaders of small businesses who want to make that next big step up in profitability but are hampered by following too closely in the former owner's footsteps, not stepping back to reassess how they're running things or getting stuck in a start-up, austerity mind-set. Times change, businesses change, and customers' needs change, so you must change and adapt. These are just a few of the things that can stop you from growing and reaching your real capacity, both as a business and as a leader.

The stories I share are personal and real. As you progress through the book you will see the changes that happened, the growth, the understanding, and the learning. Nativity grows up. Boys become men, girls become women. Success follows failure. A change of attitude saves the day. I wanted you, the reader, to know that we are real people experiencing real-life issues. My hope is that you too can learn something here and apply it to your business and avoid some of the inevitable pitfalls that are surely in your future.

"The best way to predict the future, is to create it."

—*Peter Drucker*

CHAPTER ONE:

Restarting Up—Your Business 2.0

My dad was a Greek immigrant and a former ship's captain. He was one of the youngest captains to be awarded such a post in the Greek merchant marines, and then he sailed as captain of the *Euritan* with Marchessini lines out of New York. Early in his career he sailed on the first super tanker in the Aristotle Onassis fleet. Dad sailed around the world many times over, and the stories could fill a book. One day he met a woman, and eventually they got married. They had his first child, me, a year later. So my dad left the sea and came to the land.

My dad started his first company, World Wide Ship Repairs in 1970, doing repairs on commercial vessels near the Brooklyn Navy Yard, where he had a machine shop. He got a lot of requests from foreign vessels for metric valves, flanges, and other components. Despite the demand, metric parts weren't easy to find. The metric system, like communism, was taboo in the United States. So my dad did what any good machine shop would do in those days: he took an American valve, modified it by welding on a piece of plate, drilled the holes to match the metric pipeline flange, and then put that valve back in service. Recognizing that there was an opportunity here, he started finding suppliers and manufacturers overseas, in Europe and in Asia, and bought these metric products to put a few on his shelves. Sales grew quickly; by 1985, World Wide Metric was born out of World Wide Ship Repairs.

As a kid, I worked at World Wide Ship Repair in the summertime, and by the time I graduated high school, my dad had sold off all the assets of his first business and poured them into the new company, World Wide Metric. We served the commercial shipping market through regional suppliers called *ship chandlers*, who would become our distribution channels. That's how the business got started.

I was one of four people in the company in those early days, and I served as the gofer. I'd "go fer" this and "go fer" that. During that time, I got to see how an entrepreneur starts a business. Dad didn't start his business by creating mission or vision statements about attitudes or values, as we often see and read about in new companies. The genesis of the business was his blood, sweat, and tears. He instilled his work ethic in me during those early years. I saw firsthand the trials, tribulations, and long hours. Dad would spend weekends at the office just trying to build the business, and every single dollar he ever made was put right back into inventory. Whenever we kids would ask my mother for things, she used to always say that we couldn't afford them. Growing up, I always thought that we were poor because every dollar that was made went back into growing the business.

The company grew quickly, and in 1989, we opened up our first satellite office in Houston. We were fortunate to have our expansion timing coincide with an existing vendor pulling out of the market. A deal was made, and business increased sharply. Then in 1991, we decided to open up the California office. I opened and managed the branch there, still going to college at night. I was doing the earliest marketing for our company and found the experience of making day-to-day decisions empowering, but I soon realized that it wasn't enough for me. I wanted to grow, and the only way I saw to do that was to go out and sell. My father did not especially like salespeople per se, and the idea of chasing business seemed tacky to him on some level. I just felt that we weren't at our ceiling; our business hadn't grown much and was stagnating. We had reached a plateau.

I'd grown up in the business and had absorbed a lot of my father's philosophy on how things should be done along the way, but a big part of me wasn't sure that the work was for me. I thought that maybe I needed to do something different—to see other things. In California, I got a chance to explore other businesses and talk to a lot of people. When I came back to the home office in 1996, I was a different person; I was a lot more confident in what I believed in and in what I believed to be right, and my father was at the height of his game. We were two bulls thrusting their ideas at each other, and I realized that one of us had to give—and it wouldn't be him. So I left, determined to steer my own course and make my own way.

In late 1997, I got involved with Dale Carnegie Training, which was a major shift for me. I had the opportunity to conduct training with numerous companies, hear numerous leader ideas, and see business from a different perspective. During my time at Dale Carnegie, I was a successful sales instructor and sales representative. I not only replaced the income I'd been earning previously; I surpassed it. Within a year, I was in the top 500 in sales, and by my second year I was in the top 250 and well on my way to greater success.

It was just at this time that my father and brother sat down with me and discussed my returning to the family business. We all agreed that it would be a great opportunity to take what I had learned and apply it to our company. I told them what I believed we could achieve. As a result of our conversations, my father stepped aside and named me CEO and my brother president of World Wide Metric.

Immediately after I became CEO, my dad did one of the most honorable things anybody could possibly do: he took himself off of the payroll. Even though he was still one of the owners, he was making a point. He did not want to burden the company with his payroll if he was no longer contributing to the day-to-day activities. I know this could not have been an easy decision for him. It was a risky play, placing his life's work in the hands of his kids. Either he fancied himself a hero who would one day swoop in and save our asses, or he saw something in us and put all of his faith behind us. I'd like to believe that it was the latter.

MOVING TOWARD VERSION 2.0

"Live as if you were to die tomorrow, learn as if you were to live forever,"

—*Professed Ghandi*

When my father started his business, the idea of company *values* or *mission* would have seemed very odd to him. His mission, as far as he was concerned, was to keep the business afloat, and his values became the company's values. Whenever my brother or I questioned how things were done or brought up things we felt we could improve on in terms of how we did business, my father's response was always the same: "Just get back to work." He didn't sit down with us and say, "Okay, these are our business values. This is how we do things, and this is our brand, etc."

My dad never spoke of corporate values or the vision and mission of the company. I don't think that was a very popular thing to do in those days, but it has become popular over time as people have started recognizing the value in those things. There were companies out there who did put work and thought into things like corporate values and mission statements; I realized this while watching their commercials and advertising because their brands started to speak to me. But what was our brand? What was our mission? What were our values?

In taking over the company, I recognized that there were, in fact, values implied in the way we did things in our business. We had a certain work ethic instilled in us, for instance, and we had certain ideas about humility. We were respectful. To my father, a former captain, respect was a very important thing, and being disrespectful was something that wasn't tolerated at work or at home. Growing up, you take that on just by proximity. That's not to say that it wasn't challenged—because it was, painfully so at times.

Another value that was instilled was that of learning. I remember how, when computer systems were first introduced in a general way to businesses, my father got an office computer and literally stayed up night after night, teaching himself to run it. Ultimately, it was used to manage all aspects of the business, from inventory to receivables and payables.

The metric system itself, while familiar to the rest of the world, was a relatively new and under-adopted concept in the USA. We were dealing with new product all the time and with new customers all the time. Most of the time, people were calling us. They didn't understand what they had or what they wanted. We didn't know what they had or what they wanted, so we had to work with them to try to identify their needs. It became this process of investigation, if you will; as we were figuring out the questions to ask, we were learning along with them.

This constant process of learning was certainly a core family value. Dad had bought us the full set of the *Encyclopaedia Britannica* and was an avid reader. This was our Google back in the day. On Sunday mornings you'd always find him sitting in the living room with the *Encyclopaedia Britannica* open on his lap, reading. At some point, he'd sit us kids down and ask, "Do you know anything about turbo chargers or thermodynamics?" or whatever topic he was reading about that day. Then he'd explain to us what he'd read. His lifelong thirst for learning and teaching is one that I share today, and it became central to our notions of how a business should be run. You must constantly be learning.

As a child of a business owner, I'd seen that there was no line that separated the family from the business; when Dad came home from work, work came home with Dad, and vice versa. This, unfortunately, resulted in us bringing family elements and family-type conversations into the work environment.

But to me, I always looked at the work environment as a professional environment and tried to keep a sense of separation between it and family. Even in those early days, when I wasn't in the warehouse, I would wear a shirt and tie and sometimes a suit to work because I felt like we needed to be professional and that I needed to act professionally. I knew that the bickering that went on between family members wasn't good or appropriate; other businesses didn't work that way. I thought that somehow we were unique, although I came to find out later that this was not the truth.

Even so, when it came to running the business, if my brother or sister and I differed about something, that wasn't something we would hash out in front of our team. We would not have those arguments; we would not make those faces; we wouldn't do those silly, childish things that families do without caring about what others might think . . . yeah right!

Now don't get me wrong; we joke around all the time. But I think we've successfully made clear the distinction between how family members should and should not act in front of other people. That agreement helped establish a more professional culture because the culture of the company up until then was more by default than by design. Even so, we've ended up creating an extended family atmosphere because that's what our genesis was. And whether we liked it or not, we were a family and a family business, and we still are . . . because, guess what? We spend more of our time at work with our coworkers than we do with our own families at home. So work becomes our family away from our family and part of who we are.

CHANGING OUR MIND-SET

When my father still ran the company and was trying to train me, I remember a couple of times, early on, when I'd be talking to a customer on a phone, and Dad would be sitting right next to me, coaching me through the call. If I said the wrong thing, he'd sigh, very audibly—so loudly, in fact, that the customer would ask, "What was that in the background?" I would cringe because it was embarrassing and stressful to learn in that situation—but it was also part of my growing up. I had to go through those hiccups to figure things out. My dad is a straightforward, to-the-point kind of man. Even though he was less than politically correct from time to time, he was honest and fair: characteristics that more leaders should possess today.

In those days we were learning by doing because there were no training platforms. We didn't have an HR department. We didn't have a trainer to teach us how to do our jobs; we were figuring it out as we went. Today, I can't imagine working with my new sales staff on phone calls and saying, "Ah, geez. I can't believe you just said that," while one of them was still talking to a customer. I wouldn't have many salespeople left if I conducted training in that way, so we spend a lot more time now developing people and spending time with them up front.

Today, we have our new salespeople go through several weeks of training before they speak to a customer on the phone. They've been in role-play training, learning to deal with various scenarios. They also spend at least a week in the warehouse learning hands on what we deliver to our customers. This is a critical and meaningful experience. But in the early days, we didn't really have that option; when you only have a team of one or two salespeople and you hire a third, that person is forced, out of necessity, to sink or swim. There's no real training and development; there's just, "Get in there and do it, figure it out as you go; learn by doing, listening, and learning, and eventually you'll get it."

Today, it's still not perfect; there is still the element of sink or swim, and there are a lot more products to contend with. So it's complicated, but it's working. We are always looking for ways to improve our training and onboarding processes.

MAKING IT *YOUR* BUSINESS

The above was my experience in taking over our family business. Even if you've purchased a business from someone outside your family, you're probably coming up against policies put in place by an original leader who ran the business in a very personal way, and it's likely that you will experience many of the same kinds of challenges. As my father has always said, "Where you are, I was. Where I am, you will be."

I've seen second-generation business owners working through transitions almost seamlessly, as a result of good communication and willingness to change. I've also witnessed much more challenging transitions. Some resulted in fighting, backstabbing, and even lawsuits. Emotions run deep, people's blood, sweat, and tears are poured into the entity, and it becomes difficult to maintain perspective on why we are in the business in the first place. One element that is essential during times of transition is trust; whether you're surrounded in business by family or otherwise, it is important to have trusting relationships with the good, capable people around you.

EVEN AS YOU MOVE INTO THE FUTURE, RESPECT THE PAST

Entrepreneurs often start a business because they are impressively skilled in and passionate about something. Although they are very talented in a specific area, entrepreneurs might not have the skills required to effectively run a business, such as creating and maintaining budgets, delegating tasks, managing others, and communicating ideas and information. As they develop their businesses, they often find that they are able to spend less and less time doing the very thing they were so passionate about when they started the business.

Because they are doing all the things that they hate to do, rather than the thing they love, these entrepreneurs can become disenchanted, and their businesses suffer. The business stagnates, so the entrepreneur sells it or passes it along to somebody else. The person who buys or becomes the new head of a business is, as a result of his or her knowledge and experience, likely very confident in his or her ability to make improvements. Some former owners stay on at a company after they sell it (for instance in an R&D capacity), and while they can be valuable assets, they can also become contentious when they see the new leadership coming in and running the business differently.

The fact is, whether you're buying a business that's set in its founder's ways or stepping into a generational business, these types of transitions can be difficult, and you can't always manage them on your own. There has to be a clear reality check, and sometimes it's hard to do that by yourself. Most people don't want to spend money on consultants or coaches, but sometimes you need someone with more experience to come in and provide an unbiased evaluation of how you're running things. There is inevitably going to be some preexisting baggage that might prevent you from making the changes you believe are necessary.

Even when there are serious problems that need fixing, coming in like a hammer and banging down the nails is not likely an approach that will work in the long run. As the new business owner, be sure that you're cognizant of the organization's history because that history is the essence of the company. The entrepreneur who started the company probably did so because it was something he or she believed in. It's not a matter of just coming in and making changes. It's important to recognize the cultural fiber—the DNA of the entrepreneur—and to not just pay homage to it but to find ways to weave it into your plans as you develop and grow the business.

PEOPLE SKILLS COME FIRST

The number-one skill that any business leader needs to learn is how to deal with people. People are what drive everything at World Wide Metric. Yes, we are a distribution company selling metric products, but it's our people that do the selling. It's our people that are our culture. It's people who are our customers, our vendors, and our families. People are everything in business.

My dad is a very giving and generous man who always treated everyone fairly, no matter who they were; sometimes I thought that he was being too fair and that some people didn't deserve it. But at the same time, he showed me a couple of things I didn't realize I was learning through that whole process: how to deal with people and that a leader must be fair. Business has to be a win/win situation for it to work, and to me, a win/win means being equitable to the party you're working with. The last thing you want is for people you're dealing with to walk away feeling like they got ripped off or that you got the better of them. That's not fair, and that's not going to be in your best interests.

In addition to the values I learned from my dad, I also learned a lot about how to treat people from Dale Carnegie's classic book *How to Win Friends and Influence People*. The fundamental values that Carnegie speaks about in that book are things that I still practice and talk about today. Take, for instance, the simple act of smiling; it's amazing how a smile can affect how you interact with other people. Take the time to be interested in other people because in order to be interesting, you need to be interested—a simple fact that is lost on many. We've all been around those people who are all about me, me, me. Not only are they boring, but they come across as egomaniacs. Compare that to someone who asks you a lot of questions and is curious, interested, and paying attention to your conversation—not just looking at his or her watch or over your shoulder for somebody else to speak with. People who share smiles easily and are genuinely interested in others are much more likely to form genuine relationships and, as a result, experience success in business.

Remembering names is a fundamental piece of building successful relationships because to most people, their name is the most important word. When someone calls you by the wrong name, it's obvious that he or she wasn't paying attention when you shared it. When someone does remember your name, you get the sense that he or she cares about who you are and values meeting you. When interacting with others, remember the Golden Rule: treat others as you would like to be treated. Or better yet, treat them the way *they* want to be treated.

Chapter One Takeaways:

Read: *How to Win Friends and Influence People* **by Dale Carnegie**

1. Focus your attention on people. All people. All the time. Be present in every moment because it's all about people.
2. Be fair and respectful. It will enhance your reputation and character.
3. Be in a state of constant and never-ending learning; that's how you improve.

CHAPTER TWO:

Building Momentum, Developing Growth

Back in the day, my dad always used to tell us, and still does, that the fox that chases one rabbit comes home with one, and the fox that chases two rabbits comes home with none. My father believed that this philosophy held true for World Wide Metric because our market was limited to the marine industry and, more specifically, to marine clients that needed metric products, of which there were a limited number of in the United States. So we knew that growing and expanding our company into other markets would be a challenge. Where would we start looking?

But despite the challenges and looming questions, we were determined to grow. We were passionate about expanding to new markets; we just had to figure out how to do it. We were willing to try anything, and we did. We went through our entire customer database and found out whom we'd sold to in the past and what they did. Interestingly, not all our customers were in maritime industries; they were from many different market segments. We had sold to a company that built trains, one that was in the aeronautics industry, and companies from the automotive and manufacturing industries. We even had customers who maintained the Hoover Dam. Pretty cool.

All I could think was, why are they finding us? In an attempt to answer this question, we analyzed our customer base to identify trends and make predictions about how we might further grow our business. Because our customers were coming to us from far and wide, we started to market directly to a broad range of potential customers via fax blasts and direct mail—a classic shotgun approach. Today, we've honed in on some very clear market segments, and the customers we serve fall into three major categories.

The first category is the marine market, a broad group that includes all the ship chandlers and suppliers, the vessel owners and operators, the management companies, the cruise lines, the offshore rigs, the shipyards and boatyards, the yacht yards, and the yacht companies. We cast anything that floats into the "marine bucket."

The second category is the fluid power market, which makes sense; we were already selling hydraulic fittings and tubing to the marine market. We partnered with one of our manufacturers, CAST S.p.A. (based out of Italy), which had a unique product that would help us gain entry to the fluid power market. We pitched the product to General Motors (GM), and they were very interested. Up to that point, GM only had one other brand stipulated as an approved brand: Parker Hannifin, a gigantic, multibillion-dollar conglomerate. That pitch started our foray into the industrial fluid power market and helped us achieve status as the second GM-approved vendor in that space. Our successful entry into this industry is a perfect example of why you should never ask why—instead, ask why not.

Our third market segment is the industrial market, a big bucket of all the various industries we serve but couldn't market to if we tried. The business from this segment happens organically when customers, for example from Germany, where metric is the standard, set up plants or facilities in the US, and they come to us instead of going back to Europe to pull the components they need. They find our company on the Internet and become our customers. It's nothing we could have planned for, but we were there and ready to work to keep their business.

THE THREE PILLARS OF BUSINESS GROWTH

Identifying sources of new growth, as we eventually did, is an essential step to continued growth. When an enterprise first starts out, the idea behind the business is of solving a specific problem for a specific type of customer. Only some of those enterprises realize, after some time, that a broader business potential may exist. Jay Abraham, an absolute genius of a man, has inspired me and generated millions, if not billions, of dollars of revenue and profits for many companies. Jay's famous concept is that there are only three ways to grow a business.

The first way is to *increase the number of customers you deal with*, whether it's regionally, nationally, or internationally (depending on what kind of business you have). This means identifying markets that you do not currently sell to and that could benefit from your products and/or services. You may find, as we did at World Wide Metric, that your customer data can help you identify those who are interested in what you offer but who may not have been part of your initial target market.

The second way you can grow your business is to *increase the size of the purchases your customers make*, for instance, "Do you want fries with that shake?" Offering additional or complimentary items was one of the key methods that helped us grow. We sell valves and flanges, and we recently added gaskets to our catalog. We can also add nuts and bolts, so we're basically a turnkey valve, flange, and connection solution.

The third way to grow your business is to *sell more frequently*. If you're selling to customers once a month, how could you sell to them twice a month? If you're selling to them once a year, how could you sell to them two, three, or four times a year?

You don't have to focus on all three methods of growth. You could just focus on one, and acquiring new customers is a great place to start. But in that process, you can't afford to lose sight of your existing customers. When focused on seeking new business, failing to properly service old business is a big mistake that a lot of companies make, and it can cost you valued relationships. If you start out with, "Well, we need to grow our business. Let's just go get a whole lot more customers," but don't add the infrastructure to support that expansion, you risk growing faster than you can handle. Your new customers will remember the poor service and stay away, your old customers will be annoyed that they can't reach their reps anymore, and both will begin to look elsewhere. Sometimes demand will outstrip supply. Every time we run out of stock or don't have something for our customers, we're leaving the door wide open for our competition to come in and earn the business of our good customers because we failed them.

In our business, we saw that when customers were flooding in, we would suddenly find ourselves stretched too thin in terms of inside salespeople or customer service people. We hustled to ramp up that side and made sure that we had enough people, but then we realized that we didn't have enough *knowledgeable* people who were able to deliver the same quality of service that our longtime staffers were providing. As a result, a training and development gap became apparent.

When you take your eye off one ball, another will drop, so it's important to learn how to juggle all aspects of the business. In the short term, generating revenue is a relatively easy thing to do, as is acquiring new customers. The hard things are keeping customers happy and keeping inventories where they need to be in order to serve those customers quickly.

DON'T FEAR FAILURE

It's inevitable that you will hit speed bumps in your business because failures are often necessary for success. A lot of people think that the opposite of love is hate, and that's not true. The opposite of love is not caring. You can hate what someone did; that doesn't mean you don't love them anymore. But if you stop caring, that's the true opposite of love. The same thing goes for failure. The opposite of failure is not success; failure is the path to success, and sometimes it takes the pain of failure to find a solution and overcome that failure to experience success. You have to fail first in order to succeed. Many people try to avoid failure and never understand why they aren't successful—it's because they avoided risking failure. They never tried anything new or worked hard enough to stretch their bounds and limits, so they sit there in the status quo.

They say that it's darkest right before the dawn. The same goes for success: sometimes we experience our darkest hour just before the universe of success opens up to us. In that hour, many will simply give up hope and succumb to the darkness—big mistake. The ability to see success in failure is what Thomas Edison saw in the light bulb. If it was not for his fortitude to try just one more time, he would have never succeeded after discovering the thousand ways *not* to make it a reality. It was because of those failures that he found success. The light bulb is one of a million examples of how challenging the assumptions, the establishment, and modern-day understanding can lead to discovering a new pathway. This is the road to success, and more people should explore it. The reality is that most don't have the stomach for this path, and that is understandable. Failure is often accompanied by ridicule, disbelief, and distain. Thank god for those who don't necessarily care what others think—otherwise innovation would have died centuries ago, and we would still be using candles for lighting.

> Thank god for those who don't necessarily care what others think—otherwise innovation would have died centuries ago, and we would still be using candles for lighting.

If you want to succeed in anything, you have to be willing to fail your way to the top—to make every mistake in the book as you go. You have to fumble the ball. You have to piss somebody off. You have to underestimate. You have to overestimate. You have to overpromise. You have to under deliver. You have to not call back. You have to be late. You have to miss the tackle, miss the block, miss the putt, slice it, hook it, shank it, and hit it fat. Ship the wrong product or ship it to the wrong location. Yes, it's painful when your own mistakes hang you out to dry. But it's not a bad thing, and it's also not a permanent thing. It's only temporary. I think it's important that people embrace failure because it's the only way to get to success.

Everybody knows Michael Jordan is one of the very best players to ever grace a basketball court. What most people don't know is that he got cut from his high school basketball team as a freshman. That must have felt like a devastating failure, but look at the success he created from that experience. There are many stories like his out there: in business, sports, the arts—in every endeavor. There is a root of greatness in every success story, and it typically starts with a failure—sometimes a massive one.

IT'S NOT REAL UNTIL YOU WRITE IT DOWN— THE ART OF GOAL SETTING

Napoleon Hill's *Think and Grow Rich* is where I got my passion for goal setting and writing things down. It started in my twenties with a little day planner; I remember writing down a whole list of things I wanted, starting with a new car and stretching into income and travel—it was my bucket list at the time. Then I think two or three years went by, where I all but forgot about that list, and I happened to open that book again.

And wow—the income number that I had written down—I was checking it off. The places I wanted to travel to—I was checking those off. I was driving the car I'd wanted; a bunch of those things had actually come to fruition, and I was flabbergasted. From that day forward, I became a huge goal-setter, and everybody who knows me knows that. At one point, I even drafted a list of what I wanted from a relationship and what I wanted my wife to be like. It's amazing how the universe will align to help you achieve things and bring about those things once you make it tangible and real by writing it down. And yes, my wife embodies most if not all of those qualities I wrote down in my journal that day.

A goal is simply steps toward a worthy objective.

Many are familiar with the SMART acronym: make your goals **specific, measurable, attainable, relevant, and time based**. That's one philosophy. Brendon Burchard talks about creating DUMB goals: **dream driven, uplifting, method friendly, and behavior triggered**. Mark Murphy has a great book called *HARD Goals*: his acronym is **heartfelt, animated, required, and difficult**. This combination not only helps you get there, but it makes sure that once you are there that it is the right place for you. This will help make your goals achievable and into reality. The act of simply writing them down is a great first step. Goals are simply mile markers on the path to your ultimate destination. You will know that you are on the right path when you recognize the mile markers you pass.

In our business, we created what I call the *must-do, should-do, could-do goals* and added stretch goals, or as Jim Collins calls them, Big Hairy Audacious Goals (BHAG). On the sales side, our must-do revenue number for next year is a fixed percentage over last year's. Our must-do target is 15 percent revenue increase. We ramp up the should-do target a little higher, to 25 percent. Our could-do target is 35 percent, and our BHAG is double that. We've had our should-do years. We've had our could-do years, but we've never had a BHAG year. But as I look back at our history, I can see exactly where we're going to be in a five- to eight-year time frame. I can see this because of how we set our goals and write them down, and every seven years or so we double and hit a BHAG number.

I also believe that you can have too many goals. As a company, you need to be focused and unified behind very targeted and specific goals. If you're going after too many rabbits, you're going to come home with none. The idea here is that there should be one overarching goal that you want to accomplish in a one- to three-year time frame. It takes time.

There are many details that go into achieving your overarching goal, whether it's specifically to increase your number of customers or, more generally, to increase profitability or productivity. You can't just say, "We're going to do such-and-such and we'll automatically get there." There's a laundry list of tasks that need to be completed and points you need to reach along the way. Each quarter, you need to hit certain targets to be sure that, by the end of the year, you're going to be on track to make that overarching goal. So you can't just say in January, "I want to increase 15 percent," and then on December 31, say, "Well, we didn't hit our number, I wonder what happened?" You have to set and meet targets that measure your progress every week, month, and quarter along the way.

Now, this is not rocket science by any means, but how many of us out there actually do the work that needs to be done to outline the mile markers and the smaller, incremental goals that lead you to your ultimate goal?

The trick to making this work is to work backward. If I want to increase revenue by 15 percent by December 31, I start there and march backward through the fourth quarter. What do I need to accomplish in that fourth quarter, and the third quarter, and the second quarter, and in this very first quarter? I need to start calculating target numbers. Once I have the number, what industry sector or market vertical is it going to come from? Which particular customers do I know have the potential to yield that business? What product segments do I need to promote? What do we need to start doing? What do we need to stop doing? Who do I need to add to my infrastructure? Create quarterly themes and routines so that everyone is harmonized and focused on the attainment of the goal. Focus on the one rabbit for that quarter: What is the one rabbit we want to catch—what is the one thing that we need to get done this quarter to stay on course? If we're off course, what do we need to do to quickly get back on course?

I'll talk more later about my personal goal setting, which I feel is equally important to developing yourself as a leader.

THE POWER OF BUSINESS JOURNALING

I also keep a journal specifically about business. I started keeping my own business notes because I was one of those guys who would use the yellow pad and sticky notes, and I had papers flying everywhere. I couldn't keep track of anything to save my life. But since that time, I've learned from guys like Jim Rohn, who says of journaling, "If it's worth living, it's worth recording."

I have fourteen or fifteen journals on my bookshelf. Some of them cover more than a year. Some cover less than a year, and some are a year in two books. I used to go back every once in a while and reread the journals from the previous couple years; two years ago, I went back and read thirteen of the books from front to back. It was amazing; I thought, *Who is that guy? What the heck was he thinking and doing?* In the journals, I wrote down my business ideas, new products I wanted to have, customers I wanted to focus on, quarterly goals that I wanted to achieve, or trade shows I was visiting. I also have marketing and sales ideas and strategies in there. A lot of it is just bullet points or notes I took during meetings, on the plane, in the car—anywhere I am, so is my journal. My journals became my business notebook for all things.

THE MOST IMPORTANT THING

As a leader, you need to constantly be asking yourself the big impact questions, starting with, "What is it that I need to accomplish that's going to make this quarter successful?" And depending on what your goals are, the next question is, "Does this facilitate me moving closer to what I want to achieve, or does this move me further from what I want to achieve?" Creating a goal is great, and it feels good to be crushing your to-do list, but are you working on the right to-dos? If you're a business owner and entrepreneur, this is an opportune time to look at those things and ask, "Am I doing the most important thing today? Is the thing that I'm doing right now really serving a purpose? Am I actually moving the company forward with this particular action or activity? Is this something that someone else could do so that I'd have time to take care of something else that someone else *can't* do?" As I am asking myself these questions, I am sure to capture my ideas and thoughts in my journal. You cannot predict when a good idea will present itself, so it is always best to be prepared to capture it.

I like to think in terms of quarters, and when working in those ninety-day windows, you have a finite amount of time to get something accomplished. Things don't happen in a day, and a lot of things don't necessarily happen in a week. That's why focusing on ninety-day increments has made a significant change in our organization.

I have a page in my business journal that shows my trade shows and my marketing plans, broken down by month. I keep a "Stop Doing" page, a "Start Doing" page, a "Business Issues" page, a "Growth Ideas" page, a "Product Development" page, a "Personal Goals" page, a "Professional Goals" page, a "Company Goals" page, a "Customer Contact" page, a "Vendor Contact" page a "Trade Show" page, and a "Golf" page (yes, to keep track on where and whom I played and plan to play). I have recently added pages like a "My Excuses" page, an "Ideas" page, and a "Relational Capital" page, and I have a new monthly page, as well as an "I will, I must, I did" page. Feel free to make up your own.

I don't fill out the pages right from the get-go. I just write those topics at the top and from time to time, whenever I sit down with my journal, I flip through the pages and an idea will come to me. I'll think of something I should start or stop doing, or a marketing or growth idea, and I'll make a note of it on the appropriate page. I have a specific place where I can make a particular note; instead of just opening up to a random page, there are set pages that I have designated for that specific information.

When I look back in my old journals, I might check off some things that I was thinking of executing back in 2005. That's a really cool feeling—to see something and say, "Oh yeah. I actually did that last year. I just didn't go back to check off that one part yet." It's satisfying to see progress in black and white.

I like to think that journaling and goal setting are the key things that help to propel us because if you don't have any sort of tactical plan in place or targets that you want to hit, it's easy to let things slide. All of my journals and goal writing have the same purpose: to help me focus on the series of tasks that will take me and my business where we want to go—mile by mile, choice by choice.

Are you being mindful about your goals? About your progress? About your setbacks? It's amazing how much you can learn by looking back at your journals and lists of past goals. It's amazing how much you can achieve. The best part is going back and rereading those journals and seeing the person in that moment in time as well as the growth and learning that have since taken place.

But journaling is only useful if you begin writing. The best time to plant a tree was twenty years ago; the second-best time is today. So go get a journal, and start recording your ideas and thoughts. Next year is coming, as is the next decade—whether you like it or not. Begin journaling today. You will be amazed in ten years.

Chapter Two Takeaways:

Read: *Think and Grow Rich* by Napoleon Hill, *Good to Great* by Jim Collins, and *The Sticky Point Solution* by Jay Abraham

1. Buy a journal.
2. Use it to take notes in all your meetings.
3. Write down your goals, your plans, and your ideas.
4. Title several pages separately for specific information (i.e. "stop doing" page) and leave the space blank below to add ideas as they come up.
5. Don't just ask why, ask *why not?*

STOP DOING

_____

_____

_____

_____

_____

_____

START DOING

_____

_____

_____

_____

_____

_____

BUSINESS ISSUES

_____

_____

_____

_____

_____

_____

GROWTH IDEAS

_____

_____

_____

_____

_____

_____

PRODUCT DEVELOPMENT

_____

_____

_____

_____

_____

_____

PERSONAL GOALS

_____

_____

_____

_____

_____

_____

PROFESSIONAL GOALS

_____

_____

_____

_____

_____

_____

COMPANY GOALS

_____

_____

_____

_____

_____

_____

CUSTOMER CONTACT

_____

_____

_____

_____

_____

_____

VENDOR CONTACT

_____

_____

_____

_____

_____

_____

TRADE SHOW

_____

_____

_____

_____

_____

_____

GOLF

_____

_____

_____

_____

_____

_____

MY EXCUSES

IDEAS

RELATIONAL CAPITAL

_____

_____

_____

_____

_____

_____

MONTHLY

_____

_____

_____

_____

_____

_____

I WILL...

_____

_____

_____

_____

_____

_____

I MUST...

_____

_____

_____

_____

_____

_____

I DID...

Taking the Reins

One of the phrases I heard a long time ago that I really love is the definition of *luck* as "where preparedness meets opportunity." In Earl Nightingale's book, *Lead the Field*, he talks about "the field of diamonds." A farmer becomes so enthralled with the idea of diamond mining that he decides to sell his farm and go on a hunt for diamonds, and he spends the rest of his life hunting for diamonds all over the world. He ends up dying poor. Meanwhile, the new owner was down by the river on the farm, and he found these marvelous-looking stones. He took them back to his house and displayed them. A guest noticed the stones and asked the farmer, "Where did you get them?" They were raw diamonds in their natural state, and that farm turned out to be one of the largest, richest diamond fields in all of Africa. You might very well be sitting on your own field of diamonds.

In my world, I see diamonds (and opportunity) everywhere, so when my father asked me to come back and run the family company, I was enthusiastic about it. Some of the first things I learned were the concept of profit, what profit really was, and how a business operates within a certain range of operational capital. That was the biggest business lesson I learned in taking the reins. You would think that this is something that I would have already had under my belt, but I certainly did not understand cash flow. I didn't have a clear understanding of what differentiated cash flow from profit, at least, not enough to understand the bottom line of a profit and loss (P&L) statement. Many business owners are focused on other aspects of the business and neglecting the cash. They rely on people like accountants to basically tell them what their P&L is.

Consider your checking account. There's money coming in, and there's money going out. The balance is what's left over. So from month to month, is your cash position increasing or decreasing? Are you always in the negative? Is your bank always calling you because you're overdrawn? These are things I knew about, but applying it to business was a little bit different because I got so focused on the P&L statements: I'd see revenue, and I'd see the cost of goods being subtracted. Then we take our expenses out of that amount, and we were left with a bottom line. When we had profitable bottom lines, month by month, I just assumed that meant we had cash in the bank.

At our company, my brother is the president, and I'm the CEO. People ask us, "How do you guys divvy up the business?" We often joke that I bring in the money, and my brother spends the money. That's how we split up the operational aspect of the company because my strength is revenue generation, and his is managing the cash that flows in and out of the business.

One of the first things we came to terms with was having to adjust our end-of-year Christmas bonus. We had a long tradition of giving the bonuses to everyone to share in the good year, but as we grew, we had more people on our team to give these bonuses to. We had to rethink how we were going to do this. My dad had taught us at a very young age to not operate with other people's money. Our business started with the capital of the entrepreneur who began it. A lot of other businesses start on a shoestring too, but some wind up borrowing money from the bank to meet payroll or expenses. So we simply had to put our people first and pay them before we paid ourselves. Granted, we had to wait several months before we could cash our own checks, even though we were showing enough profit on the books to pay for them at the end of the year. We didn't act on credit. We did everything from within, so the cash that we had was the only cash we had to work with. For the better part of fifteen years or so, that's what our mind-set was. In those early days, we had some profit, but we always left money in the company first. So we had to wait for enough cash to build up again. This led to my first lesson, which was to ask, "Well, why don't we have the cash? Where is it?"

We did some digging, and that's when we realized that our customers had the cash—*our* cash. We were selling product. We were improving the business. But what we quickly realized was that we had some customers who were slower payers, and that trickle-down effect was impacting us. We had customers who were carrying hundred-plus day receivables; some of our customers were carrying six months of receivables, if not longer.

At that point we said, "Wait a second. What are our terms?" Our terms were thirty days . . . or so we thought. We told everyone, so why weren't they paying in that time frame? We started to talk to customers, and of course you heard stories like, "Well, you know, my customer didn't pay me, so I can't pay you until they pay me," indicating that they, too, were cash-strapped. That's when my brother and I realized that we needed to change the way we did business.

We learned how to change our cash flow situation from the One-Page Strategic Plan in Verne Harnish's *Mastering the Rockefeller Habits*. In the book, Harnish talks about how cash is like oxygen for a business and that it's the one thing you can't do without for any length of time. Without cash, a business has no oxygen to breathe, especially if it's growing.

We've learned that growth requires a whole lot of cash "oxygen." If you don't have enough of it, the pace at which you can grow is limited, if not stalled altogether. We wanted to grow the business, but we quickly learned that couldn't be done without cash. You don't want to borrow, because as soon as the banks have their hands in your pocket, they never leave. That's not the way to grow a business. You don't want to be reliant on anybody else. Our father had taught us that you want to be self-sufficient.

Any business owner-operator in business today is not only the revenue generator—the key person—but they're also probably the key collector. And they hear the same stories; it's either, "The check's in the mail," or, "Hey, we've known each other a long time. Give me a little time, and I'll get you your cash." Eventually, they do take care of it but not without a lot of effort, and the fact of the matter is that it's consuming. You must develop a good cash strategy, so that you can have a good amount of money in the bank because running out of capital is the one thing that can kill your business. Cash management's number-one job is to ensure the future of the company.

How did we deal with the overdue payments problem? First, we hired someone to take over accounts receivable—to be the appointed person on collection. Then we identified the worst-case customers, the ones who, at a hundred-plus days, weren't paying their bills. The goal wasn't necessarily to move them all of them from one hundred to thirty days overnight, because we knew that was impossible. It had to be gradual.

The next step was telling the really hard cases that, basically, their accounts were closed until they paid the bills. However, that's a strategy that you have to be very selective with because if you do that to everybody, your business would dry up really quickly. You not only won't have your cash, but you also won't have any customers, and that doesn't help your business. We had to make this a process—a disciplined process.

After you have a process for collecting on overdue accounts, you must also find the right person to run the collections department. I used to call ours "the saber-toothed tiger." They wouldn't back down but were willing to maintain a certain amount of flexibility to make deals. You have to negotiate and develop a relationship with the people who pay the bills.

The whole point was to improve everything just a little bit. If you had somebody paying in one hundred days, try to move that to ninety or eighty days. If you had somebody at sixty or seventy days, try to get that account down to forty or fifty. We tried to get those that were forty-five days and over down to thirty. For those who were already paying in thirty days, if there was any way to improve that—perhaps by offering them one or two percentage points for paying their bills in ten to fifteen days—it was worth giving up those two percentage points to get the cash flowing in.

SHIFTING SLOW-PAYING CUSTOMERS
TO CREDIT CARDS

The other big change that we made was to start working with a credit card company to switch our toughest-to-collect-from customers to credit card terms. That meant that with any future purchases, from that day forward, those customers started buying from us on credit cards. Those hundred-day payers became almost instant cash. The credit card companies don't pay for thirty days, but they were good for that thirty-day schedule. And that was better than a hundred days, even if the credit card company took their percentage.

That had a big impact on us. Today, 20 percent or more of our cash flow comes in via credit card companies. All first-time customers have to pay on credit card because the people who ended up abusing our terms the most weren't small companies. Sometimes they were very large companies that said, "Hey, we're a big company. We don't pay on credit cards. We want to establish credit terms." So we would get them established on terms and get a $500 order out to them, and then they would disappear into oblivion. Finding somebody to contact with our invoice to get paid took months, if not years. We were jumping through hoops to get a $500 payment, and we were spending too much time and money on calls and hourly-employee pay just to collect on that small amount. It doesn't make sense to pay more on collections than the amount due.

Credit cards quickly eliminated that problem. All orders had to be done through credit cards until we had enough time to properly evaluate the creditworthiness of a customer. We sell on need; people don't come to us because they *want* to buy a valve or a fitting. They *need* the product because their system or a project or a machine is down. Without our product, they can't move things forward, so they need us. They need the product shipped out that same day. They don't have time to play around. Sometimes they don't want to wait to establish credit terms. So now it actually works more efficiently because with the credit cards, we can get things out the door quickly and still know that we'll get paid. Our business is built on speed, so this change benefited not only us but our customers as well. We've converted many customers who were previously credit-term customers into using credit cards.

IF YOU DON'T BILL THEM, THEY DON'T PAY

We realized early on that we needed to be faster with our invoicing because we would deliver the goods to the customer, and they would have possession for over a week before we got the invoice mailed out. By the second week they'd finally get the invoice, and we wouldn't get paid for thirty more days at the earliest, if not sixty or ninety days. We were adding to the delay of the payments by not being prompt with our invoicing.

How did we revamp our invoicing process? Now, the day the order ships, the invoice is processed and sent out within twenty-four hours, often via e-mail. One idea was to print invoices on blue paper, rather than the usual yellow or white, so that when we called up an accounts payable clerk, we could just say, "Can you grab that blue invoice?" and they could easily find it. They didn't have to go rummaging through thousands of pages because ours was the only blue one in the pile.

Our accounts receivable clerk's job is to make relationships. Relationships don't only exist between seller and buyer; it is equally important that the accounting teams develop relationships. When we first do a call with the customer, we find out very quickly who the people are that we need to speak to—that is, who pays the bills. We make contact with them before the first invoice even goes out to establish that relationship and to make sure that they're clear on our terms. We also make sure that our invoices are stamped with the actual day they went out, so that the person paying it knows where they stand regarding the time frame in which they're expected to pay.

KNOW YOUR CUSTOMERS' PAYABLES PROCESSES

Some companies only pay their bills on the first and fifteenth of the month, so you have to make sure that your invoices align with your customers' payment schedules. Knowing in advance what your customers' payable habits are will allow you, as it has us, the ability to better forecast your cash flow. The aim is to work congruently and understand their processes better.

These simple processes, over time, have brought us from what was an average of seventy to ninety days on receivables down to a manageable thirty-two to thirty-five days. Even in hard times, we've held the line and remained consistent with that time frame because our customers, our relationships, and the processes we put in place have kept us moving in that direction.

DEALING WITH SLOW PAYERS

We're not afraid to put customers' accounts on hold, no matter who they are, if they're not responding. If we're not being communicated with, we'll red flag an account and let those people know, "Hey, we've attempted to e-mail and call you many times, but nobody's responded." Sometimes I end up making those calls and telling them, "I've got no problem with you paying even in forty-five or ninety days, if that's what you have to do, but you have to communicate with us because in our world, when you don't, that's a red flag." Sometimes, people don't pay bills because they're strapped for cash and going out of business, but they'll never tell you that until it's too late. You try calling them, but the phone keeps ringing, and you don't hear from anyone. So, if you don't plan at least a little, if you don't set a few goals, and if you don't set the course, then you're the only one to blame if the account goes south. Timing is everything, and it matters every day.

You can't move a hundred-day payer to a thirty-day payer overnight. Some of our long-term customers had old debt that lingered for a while, but all the new business we did with them fell under our new payment programs. A lot of times we said, "Okay. If you have X dollars in arrears, we're going to put you on a payment program for that, and you're going to pay that down, simultaneously all your new orders have to be credit card or payment in advance." That way, no new business would be added to their old ticket. Their old debt would be chiseled away, slowly but surely until the balance was zero again.

The above kind of payment plan is a tactic that we've used success-fully to help customers align with our new programs, and we could never have grown into the company we are today if it weren't for our customers and for having this process in place to help manage the cash flow. We couldn't have grown and added more products and diversified the business without the customers paying their bills, and I think that's true of every business.

BE NIMBLE, AND LOOK AT ALL YOUR OPTIONS

We're a brick-and-mortar kind of company, so everything we do is based on inventory. When I go into my warehouse, I don't just see products sitting on a shelf; I see greenbacks sitting on the shelf, collecting dust. I see investment dollars that have been accumulated, waiting there for the day that they get to find a home.

You have to always be prepared; it takes a big and growing investment to make sure you have enough of a product available when your customers needed it. Still, that's cash sitting on the shelf. When you're strapped for cash and trying to grow, you have to cut your expenses by either cutting payroll or buying less product. When the economic downturn hit in 2009, we scaled back. We didn't lay people off; we slowed our purchasing of products. We throttled back significantly on our purchase orders and reserved the cash we needed to maintain operational solvency. The only other options would have been to borrow money or increase sales, but in a declining market, we didn't have that choice. What ended up happening was that the demand for our product didn't go down. In fact, it actually increased a little bit because we're not in the new construction side of the business; we're more in the replacement side of the business. Being in replacement isn't "recession proof," but it is "recession resilient" in the sense that people still needed to fix the equipment they already had. People still needed to repair things, but they wouldn't necessarily start new construction. They would just fix something to keep it operating.

When we saw that the demand was still there, we quickly started to ramp back up. Within a year, we were right back where we had been the year before, if not ahead of that. So we didn't languish in the downturn for too long. We only dropped 15 percent revenue from one year to the next, and then, only a year later, we bounced right back to where we had been.

Time never stops flowing, and in some cases it's like the rapids. It moves so quickly that before you know it, you're out to sea, adrift and waiting for the wind to pick up so that you can return to land. That's also true of cash flow, and that's why we knew we needed to get control of it.

Some companies do not make enough profit to pay the bills. Not having a proper grasp of your cash flow can be the first nail in your business's coffin. We have evolved and now have an open line of credit but not for day-to-day, operational purposes; the line is more for opportunity purposes, like larger projects or inventory ramp-ups, or as bridge capital when needed. All the while, we're focused on getting our borrowed amount back to zero as quickly as possible. We take other people's money even more seriously than our own, and I think that is a very healthy philosophy.

Chapter Three Takeaways:

Read: *Scaling Up* **by Verne Harnish**

1. Focus on cash management. Cash is oxygen for business and your company cannot breathe without it.
2. Accounts receivable (AR) is a relationship-based position and needs focused attention.
3. Learn how to read a financial statement: take an online course or hire a CFO for the day and have them teach you. You cannot afford not to do this.

CHAPTER FOUR:

Step Back from the Hat Rack— Distractions and Diversions That Can Wreck Your Business

I think that as an entrepreneur or a business owner of any level, if you're looking to grow your business, one of the biggest things holding you back is probably trying to wear too many hats. Most entrepreneurs and young business owners are in the habit of doing it all—partly because they want to save money to put back into the business, partly because they don't know how to delegate, and partly because on some level, they simply don't trust anyone to put as much love into the work as they do. All of these are limiting beliefs, and all of them will hold you back.

You can't do it all, and you can't do it all alone. This was not a lesson my siblings and I learned in a day. It took

> You can't do it all, and you can't do it all alone.

some time to sink in. In the beginning, we were involved in every aspect of the operation, from customer calls to billing and receivables and negotiating with freight carriers. This was all encompassing and all fun, to a point. Then we got busier as more time passed. The repetitiveness of business started to seem like old hat, but we were still doing everything. After a while, there was just always too much to do; it never ended. It started to feel overwhelming at times, and then the fractures started. Things were slipping through the cracks, and stress levels were rising. It wasn't bad, but it wasn't quite good, either. We had to start hiring more people and delegating tasks and responsibilities (not an easy thing to do when you do it so well—or so we thought). We found ourselves working *in* the business, but no one was working *on* the business. We were just doing busywork in first and second gear. Were we really working in the best interest of the company and its clients? Were we really that productive, or were we just super busy?

Consider your current personal productivity: How productive are you *really* in a given day? If you look at the eight hours of a day and multiply that by sixty minutes per hour, you have 480 minutes that you're working in a day. In how many of those 480 minutes are you truly being productive, and what does that productivity really mean? Does it mean that you're taking the sales calls, writing them up, and generating a purchase order? How long does that actually take? Is it your job to make the phone call that pushes someone to the next step? How long does that actually take? Now, think about what your time is worth and how much of it you're squandering. If you start doing the math, you might be petrified at the answer.

Now, consider the employees working under you: think about their productivity. The simple fact is that there is a fixed amount of time in the day, and busywork is not productive work. I'm not saying that people are inevitably unproductive. I'm just trying to make a point:

the problem most of us have, especially in the owner and leadership roles, is that we do too much and end up not getting much done at all. More to the point, we don't get the *right* things done, and that's the imperative thing.

STOP DOING THAT: TWO KEYS FOR EXPONENTIAL PRODUCTIVITY GAINS

Fixing a productivity issue starts with you, and it's a two-step process. The first step is figuring out what you need to stop doing. I call this the "Stop Doing" list. Making that list and sticking to it is one of the most beneficial things I've done in my career. The second step is delegating.

Here's how it works: Open up a page in your business journal. If you don't already have a journal, get one, and make this your first page. At the very top of the page, write the words "Stop Doing." Then, just go through your regular day and pay closer attention to all the things that you do. You might want to take another sheet of paper and write down what you did that day, such as the tasks you performed and the calls that you made—all the activities that made up your day.

Now look at that list of everything you did. First off, what is on this list that you absolutely hate to do? What task on this list is a time sink, the delegation of which would free you up to do more important things that only you can do? Perhaps you don't do that task very well, and it would be better served under someone who loves and can do it better than you.

But maybe you're actually the only person who can do a particular task. In life and in business, there are things that we have to do. So suck it up and do it. But if a task is something that is at a different pay grade than yours, then you should delegate. Figure out who can do it, and ask that person to do it for you. There are two choices in life: you can either spend the cash to have someone else do the work, or you can do it yourself and spend your time. You can probably get more money, but you can never get more time. So you have to figure out which is more valuable to you—the money in the bank account or your time. That time spent on a task could potentially yield ten times more money than you'd spend to delegate it, if you were to use that time to do things that would better benefit your company.

THE TOP HAT

In addition to being CEO, I'm also head of sales and marketing for our organization. Even though a lot of people lump them together because they work in harmony, sales and marketing are two very distinct arenas. So if I work eight hours (or 480 minutes) a day and split my time between marketing and sales, that means I only spend 240 minutes a day—tops—on each. And that's a generous estimate that assumes I'm focusing on actually productive things rather than putting out fires, having five-minute doorway conversations, running to the bathroom, or getting interrupted by another person, whose agenda is not my own.

Truthfully, I'm lucky if I get two hours' worth of productive time in a day—and that's still split between sales and marketing. Do you think that I deserve to think of myself as the sales and marketing leader of our company? How productive am I in this business, which I own? Honestly, the answer is "not very," and it's scary to think about how unproductive I really am in those roles. Having realized that I can't do it all, I recently hired a marketing manager and a sales manager. They can each spend the 480 minutes of their days focusing their efforts in marketing and sales, respectively, so that I can oversee, manage, and provide insight. And now I can spend my 480 minutes focusing on the task at hand: being CEO of this company and focusing on those elements that only I can do—chasing that one rabbit.

As a CEO, my learning process is still ongoing—and that's after I've been at this for fifteen years, with an overall twenty-eight years in various other positions. As the company continues to grow, we're constantly looking for ways to improve, and for me, I'm personally looking for things to stop doing so that I can look for the mile markers along the road and help everybody meet those goals.

It is with this the kind of hyper-focus, chasing one rabbit, that we all need to come into tune with. It doesn't happen overnight. When I first started my "Stop Doing" list, I didn't realize where it was going to take me. One of the first things I wanted was to get out of the sales pit and stop doing day-to-day sales transactions. I used to say that I had two jobs; I'd go to work in the morning, and then at night, I'd come home and start my second shift, doing marketing until one o'clock in the morning. Then I got married, had kids, and needed to reevaluate my use of time. It's time that you can never get back, and whether it's with your family or your business or anybody else, the time slips away.

Watching my father go into his eighty-fourth year, I realized that he has lived a wonderful life and done many things. But the one thing he can never do is get more time than what's left on his clock. You have to do the best you can with what you have, and learning how to stop doing things to get back your time is of critical importance, especially for those who want to be successful. My father was a master of hyper-focus, and he always got things done.

You can't just say, "I'm going to stop marketing," and be done; you have to hire the right people. You have to train the right people. You have to cultivate the right people. You have to develop all these elements, and that takes time. I think it was eighteen months before I could honestly say that, at any given time, it had been a full week since I had been in the sales pit. And I found myself in an office, scratching my head, saying, "What do I do now?" It was the greatest day of my life when I asked myself that question. Now I'm finally able to focus on the important task of driving our business forward.

YOU'RE NOT THE BEST AT EVERYTHING— SO STOP TRYING TO BE

Part of what makes it hard for anyone running a business to delegate is the stubborn sense that no matter what the job is, you can do it better. Most people have the attitude of, "I don't have the time to sit there and teach them this. I'm going to do it myself and just get it done because I know I'll get it done right, and we can move this on. I'll teach it to them later."

Well, later never happens, and it's a mistake for both you and the employee. Keep in mind the saying, "Give a man a fish, and you feed him for a day. Teach a man to fish, and he eats for a lifetime." Building a business doesn't mean that you do it all yourself. Building a business doesn't mean that you run yourself ragged so that you are dead in the end. Building a business is building people, infrastructure, and processes so that you can lead and ultimately manage your company or hire managers to lead and run your company for you.

If you are really good at something, you should recognize what it is that you are really good at. Verne Harnish taught me this concept; he is a big believer in the idea of hiring the right people to manage your company so that you have time to take care of more important areas, such as growing your business. Verne took his own advice; he hired a president to run his company and pulled out of the day-to-day operations. He even moved abroad so that he could focus on one thing that he was good at: presenting. He is the brand, and he is the product, so he should be out there delivering the goods—not behind the scenes doing administration or management.

Harnish's story made me ask myself, what are the things that only I can do? I narrowed the list down to just a few things. For me, it's communication, both external and internal: speaking to key customers and other CEOs and doing whatever needs to be done at that level. Another area of communication is in maintaining our key vendor relationships and making sure that we are their top priority and communicating that they are our top priority. Biggest of all is communicating with my staff, whether it's with my managers or other employees, because nobody can deliver my message as well as I can. I'm still weeding out things that I'm pretty sure I could delegate, so it's an ongoing process.

As the leader, you're the one who will make the differences and make those incremental changes that, over time, will have a huge effect on both your revenue and profits. Whatever only you can do in your business is where you need to spend your time to create the biggest impact.

A lot of entrepreneurs are probably reading this and thinking that this message sounds great when you have money, but what if you are on a shoestring budget? What if you are just starting out? Again, it's a process of one thing at a time, one step at a time. You have to stop and make a little effort. Work through your processes and find ways to cut those time wasters out of your schedule so that you can focus on key components that will take you to the next level.

Just as you get your time back, you'll see that things will quickly appear to fill it up. Be protective and defensive of your time; fill it with more of what only you can do, and don't fall back into the old trap. Use your newfound time as an opportunity to grow your employees in ability and experience. That's the philosophy you have to take as a leader, as an owner, and as an entrepreneur. You have to constantly be finding ways to teach people how to fish for themselves. Sit down, and start your own "Stop Doing" list. You'll be surprised at how much you can let go of—and how much time you can reclaim for the things that demand your full attention.

THE NINETY-MINUTE MIRACLE

I still get hit with distractions and have to put out fires, but the key for me was learning to work in ninety-minute intervals during my day. The goal, initially, is to start by picking a day this week in which you want to block off, say, forty-five minutes—with the intention to build up to ninety minutes. Pick a project or something that you need to get started on but haven't been able to because you were just too busy. Turn off everything—your phone, your e-mail, and all other distractions—and concentrate, even to the point where you close your door and put a sign saying, "Busy for the next forty-five or ninety minutes. Do not disturb." Your people will respect you for doing this because if you don't manage your time, your inbox, and your phone, everyone else will, and it will all be run according to their agenda rather than yours. If you want to be proactive, if you want to be successful, if you want to move the needle, then you need to take control of your time.

The ultimate goal would be to have multiple ninety-minute segments during your day. To keep myself on task, I bought a ninety-minute countdown clock that has a start and stop button. When I'm going to start a block of time, I hit the button. After ninety minutes, the beeper will beep. I'll stop what I'm doing, no matter where I'm at, and I'll get up from my desk and walk around the office. I'll go visit a few people and then come back. And if I'm ready to go again, I'll pick up my ninety-minute clock again, and I'll get started on my next block of time. I might be carrying on with the task I already started, and if I complete that task before my ninety minutes are up, then I give myself the permission to check e-mails or to make a few phone calls for the remaining amount of time.

My biggest pet peeve is when someone comes to my door and tells me, "Hey, did you get my e-mail I just sent you?" I have sworn that the next time someone does that, I would say, "Oh, this one you sent me ten seconds ago?" and hit delete and then advise them to send it to me again and that I will respond in due time. Of course, there are emergencies and urgent matters to attend to, but sending an e-mail should never be one of them. Pick up the phone or run into my office with the fire extinguisher—then you have my attention. This may sound harsh, but you must learn to defend your time because no one else will.

Chapter Four Takeaways:

Read: *Eat That Frog!* **by Brian Tracy**

1. Create a "Stop Doing" list and stop doing those things.
2. Delegate tasks that don't require you.
3. Buy a countdown clock, and begin working in uninterrupted forty-five- and ninety-minute intervals. Shut down your email program, turn off your ringer, turn off any notification pings and dings on your smart phone, and *focus* on that one thing that you must do.
4. DO this now!

CHAPTER FIVE:

The Customers Are Always Right—
Except When They're Wrong

There are some quotes that I've lived by for a long time now, and one of them is, "Prescription before diagnosis is malpractice." I remind my team almost daily that you need to ask a lot of questions to be clear on what the customer needs because a lot of times customers don't actually know what they need, even if they've been in the business for a long time and think they do. For me, it's an ethical requirement to tell people that they might be wrong about something that they think they know a whole lot about—although it requires a sensitive approach to do so without giving offense.

My other favorite quote is a variation on the old Golden Rule, "Do unto others as you would have done unto yourself"—it's Tony Alessandro's Platinum Rule, "Do unto others as they would want done unto themselves." It's better to treat people as they would want to be treated rather than how you'd like to be treated because we're all different. In customer service, that means figuring out how to speak to people on their level or how to introduce ideas and products to them. Like most businesses, we deal with a lot of very strong, decisive personalities who can sometimes come off as arrogant or angry. The old joke around here is, "Well, who shit in his cereal today?" There's no way to know what kick-started this guy's crappy mood, but he's taking it out on you: "I need this valve, and I need it now!" You try to take him through a questioning process to ensure that he'll get what he needs, but he doesn't want to play. He's pushing you to give him an answer, and that's where the danger of "prescription before diagnosis" comes in. How do you deal with bellicose guys like this, without either caving and potentially selling them the wrong thing or letting your irritation rise to the level of theirs?

I say, "I'd love to help you with your product, but prescription before diagnosis is malpractice. I don't need a malpractice suit." That usually gets at least a chuckle and slows things down enough for us to lead the conversation back to finding the right solution. I usually get these guys after they've hung up on someone else, so it's important to cool things off at the top of the conversation. It's hard to deal with someone whose rage is turned up to eleven from the get-go, but humor works for me.

"If you're right, there is no reason to be angry. If you're wrong, you have no right to be angry." I've always loved that quote because it reminds me that yelling back—which is certainly many people's understandable, knee-jerk reaction to hostility—is no way to deal with customers (or with anyone else). Managing your emotions can be a challenge; it's hard not to take things personally when someone's yelling at you for your incompetence or your stupidity or why you're

> If you're right, there is no reason to be angry. If you're wrong, you have no right to be angry.

asking these stupid questions when you should know the answer. But the fact is that these people can't or aren't managing their emotions, and that means you have to manage yours.

Dealing with customers, one of the things that I learned very quickly was to try to stay calm. If somebody was on a rampage, the only thing I could do was to kill him or her with kindness. I've never hung up on a customer, I've never shouted back at a customer, and I've never told a customer to shut up—but I've had customers do all those things to me.

Working through the concepts of Vernon Howard, author of *Psycho-Pictography*, helped me understand how the mind works. Understanding people's psychology—that was a huge help because dealing with customers can be tough, and you must understand they are people first. Buyers in general come off as being tough people because they use muscle to get their way; it's one of the best weapons that they have. I learned from Howard to look at thoughts and emotions as things and to separate myself from them. Maybe you've experienced this yourself: someone says something, and you find yourself repeating and believing that thing. All of a sudden you find yourself regurgitating that information as if it were your own. It's not even your own thought; it's somebody else's thought that has been put into your mind, and you're out there repeating it. Who really has control over your mind? Is it you or someone else who puts a thought in your head? Is that really your opinion, or are you carrying the torch for someone else's ideas?

Early on, I used to take interactions with rude customers personally. When staff came to me crying because someone was rude or obnoxious to them, I would contact the customer and call him or her out on it: "Hey, you spoke to one of my people this way. You want to explain to me what happened here?" I let those customers know that if they want to do business with us, they need to apologize for that behavior because it was unacceptable. That may sound counterintuitive . . . isn't the customer always right? But I honestly think that standing up to tough customers makes them respect you more than lying down would.

The fact is, customers pay your bills. I do sign the checks here, but the customers are the ones who pay the payroll (my pay included), and you have to keep that in mind. I urge my staff to do the best they can and to get as many questions answered as they can because that's the critical thing that helps you solve customers' problems. At the end of the day, they'll forget the interaction and remember that you were the person and the company that helped them out with their issue, and you'll have earned that business. I had a meeting recently with one of my vendors who told me that everyone really seems to respect and enjoy working with our company because our salespeople work at establishing that rapport and supportiveness. My vendor is that much more engaged with us because of how engaged our customers are with us. The value of this is huge.

These things don't just happen overnight; they're cultivated and proven over time. You have to constantly make that attitude the forefront of who and what you are as a company when dealing with your customers.

WHAT'S THAT CUSTOMER WORTH TO YOU?

If you have a $10,000 account, don't look at them as just a $10,000 annual account; that's not how we look at customers. Instead, look at that customer's buying over a ten-year period. That $10,000 customer just became a $100,000 account. Now, how do you think about that $100,000 account? Might you think a little differently about how they want to return an item or that they're complaining about something? You might blow them off and lose that $10,000 account, but what you're really losing is a $100,000 account over the next ten years. When you start looking at customers in that way, you start treating them differently, and you start thinking about them differently. Take a look at a $100,000 account; they're a $1 million account over ten years. A million dollar account is a pretty big deal, right? By looking at accounts over a longer period of time, it changes your perspective on how you think about them. If you lost that $100,000 account this year, it may not be as significant to your overall business—but over the next ten years, that's $1 million, and that's assuming the account is going to stay at a hundred thousand dollars each year and not grow. So in reality, every customer is equally important to your business, no matter how much that account initially purchases from you. There's always a chance that a small customer can become a big customer over time. That's one of the most important things you can do to grow your business: take a small customer and turn them into a big customer. When you start scaling like that, you can see how much a customer is really worth, and that change in perspective can (and should) change how you deal with customers. Equally as important, if not more so, is to avoid being shortsighted about the effect that negative interactions with your customers can have on your bottom line.

I'll give you a perfect example: I was a huge customer of Best Buy. My family bought our TVs, our dishwasher, and our washing machine there. We bought everything that we could from Best Buy.

So naturally, when my wife needed software, she went to Best Buy. But when we loaded it into her computer, we discovered that it was a rip off; the software basically directed us to a website that required a subscription in order to make the software work on the computer. This was not stated or implied anywhere on the packaging. I felt it was a scam. We thought, "Ah, you know what, forget this, let's return this thing and get the twenty bucks back." Mind you, I've spent thousands of dollars at that store, and all I wanted was my twenty bucks back.

When I went to return it and explained why, instead of giving me my money back, they insisted that because it was open, they couldn't take the software back—and they asked me if I wanted another copy. I asked to see a manager, who just reiterated that I wasn't getting a refund. At this point, I officially became an irate customer. I started dropping F-bombs and screaming bloody murder in the middle of the store. At this point, I'd spent at least $10,000 at this store, but they were about to lose the next ten years of my purchases (likely in excess of $20,000) because they wouldn't refund that $20. That wasn't wise, because not only are they losing my business, but I am also going to tell everybody in my circle of influence about this. From a sales perspective, if you look at a consistent-spending customer such as myself in the big picture, the guy should have pulled that $20 out of his own pocket and paid me. That way he'd have retained my business. Because he didn't do that and because no one took any responsibility for it, the whole company needs a wakeup call as far as I'm concerned. That behavior is completely antithetical to how I think the sales arm of my business or any business should run. We exist to serve and solve customers' problems because when they call us, typically something's down or not working, and they need to get it back on track right then. For us, being customer-focused means solving a problem for customers and doing it quickly. The customers need to feel that we have a sense of urgency about their situation. That's what customer focus and customer service in our world looks like, and it's the same thing for most other companies.

By the way, I have not been back to a Best Buy store in over ten years, and I have told almost everyone I know that story and now you.

EMPOWERING YOUR PEOPLE TO CARE FOR THE CUSTOMER

The definition of *empowerment* is "the giving or delegation of power or authority." In management practice, it means sharing information and power with employees so that they can take the initiative to make decisions on their own to improve service and performance. When you, as a sales or customer service representative, are weighing your options, you need to ask yourself a few questions. If you or your representative can answer yes to all of the following questions, the representative should be empowered to move forward with a decision:

- Is it in the best interest of the company?
- Is it in the best interest of the customer?
- Does it follow our values?
- Is this something you're ready to take full ownership of and responsibility for the outcome?

The whole idea is to empower the people closest to the customer to be able to take care of that customer as best as your people can. Companies that put this faith in their frontline staff see big rewards in terms of customer satisfaction and loyalty. The Ritz Carlton hotel actually empowers its frontline staff to use up to $3,000 for a decision to facilitate any client's needs, and supervisors have up to $5,000 per decision. Nine times out of ten, I'm sure they don't spend anywhere near that amount, but the employees know that they are authorized to go that distance to make customers' stays satisfactory. How far do you go?

THE NEED FOR SPEED

To your customer, time is money, and nobody wants to be shunted from department to department or up the management chain to get a decision made. Nobody wants to hear, "Oh, let me go check with my manager to see if it's okay." Then they're whistling Dixie for ten minutes until someone comes back over and says it's okay. You need to empower your employees to make decisions on their own and avoid that time lag.

Early on, when I was in the sales pit, I knew I could do stuff within certain parameters. If a customer had a lower price quote from a competitor, I could try to match that quote, offer to pay the freight costs, or look for another way to make a concession. I was looking at generating business, so I played around with all sorts of configurations to get the job done—as long as they still yielded profitable transactions. Every time you tell customers that you can't do something they need done, you're driving them toward your competitors. You can't give away the farm, but you can always find ways to get creative.

It doesn't always take as much money as you might imagine. Customers are a whole lot easier to satisfy than many people think. Most companies think that most customers are trying to rip them off, and most customers think that most companies are trying to rip *them* off. But if you have a mentality of honesty, openness, and trust, chances are your customer will meet you there.

PRICE VERSUS VALUE

Sometimes a customer will come to me with lower quotes from a competitor and ask for a lower price from me. Rather than arguing the merits of my price, I can talk about the quality of the product we offer as opposed to what the competitor is quoting because sometimes it's apples to oranges. Another way to approach this situation is to ask the customer what he or she is going to do with these parts because there may be another way to solve the problem.

If your customers are quality customers, you want to keep them happy; sometimes that requires taking the time to educate them on price versus value. Sometimes, if the price is far lower than I can possibly get to, it's indicative that the parts offered by the competitor are coming from a cheap labor source that likely produces lower-quality products. Customers need to understand these quality differences so they can make an informed decision, and I need to be creative in finding ways to help them make the right choice.

YOU CAN'T CHANGE *THEIR* ATTITUDES— BUT YOU *CAN* CHANGE YOURS

If you learn to change your thoughts, you can learn to change your attitude. They say that what you think about expands, and it's true; your thoughts will attach themselves to your emotions and even to your body. It's all emotionally driven—if you squeeze a lemon, what comes out? Lemon juice. If you squeeze an angry person (of course, figuratively speaking), what comes out? Anger. It all manifests from thought.

When your customer is having a bad day, the unhappy feelings that are being squeezed out of him or her are being directed at you. As a

> If you learn to change your thoughts, you can learn to change your attitude.

company, as a sales organization, and as a customer service organization, if you're dealing with customers, you have to understand that their attitudes don't need to dictate your attitude. Just because someone is irate or angry doesn't mean that you have to respond similarly, because that gets you nowhere. It's like touching the positive end of one magnet to the positive end of another. What happens when you try to push them together? They push away from each other.

The same thing is true in all relationships—even marriage. If you want a happy marriage and you ever find yourself with one party upset or angry, the best thing you can do is shut up and listen, take it all in, and don't respond in kind. You need to let your partner cool off, and when he or she is calmer and has gotten things off his or her chest, you can sit down and have a conversation addressing the concerns. When your partner is angry, that's not a person you can deal with rationally. You have to defuse the situation.

The first thing you have to do is to let your partner know, "I understand where you're coming from. I understand your problem. I hear what you're saying." You don't want to turn around and say, "I hear what you're saying, but you're wrong." That's going to infuriate somebody that's already pissed off and angry, so the best thing to do is defuse the situation. If you can come back to it later, that's great. If not, you need to wait it out and calm your partner down to a point where you can have a realistic conversation. Your calm will spread to the other person.

It takes practice to do this. It's not manipulation but rather more of a tactic—listening and shutting your mouth—because a lot of times, we tend to want to talk too much or make statements instead of asking better questions. Telling people things doesn't necessarily help them, but asking questions that probe them and make them consider the answers—just the simple act of using the Socratic method— shows that you care enough to take an interest in them, their needs, and their thoughts.

Remember the book *Men Are from Mars, Women Are from Venus*? If a woman brings up an issue, the man typically puts on his Mr. Fix-it hat to come to the woman's aid with the approach of "Hey, honey, here's what you have to do. You have to do this, this, and this." But really, all she wanted was to just tell him how her day went because she feels emotional about it. She wants to share it with him. She doesn't want him to fix it. She just wants him to listen.

Men don't necessarily think that way. It's not that they don't care, but they don't always have the patience to listen, and this can also happen when it comes to clients. If clients call you and just want to talk, sometimes it almost turns into a therapy session where they want to vent a little about what's going on with their company. But if you don't spend that moment with the client and cultivate that relation- ship—if you just cut to the chase with, "I'm sorry you're having a bad day there, but I'm real busy here. Can you just tell me what you need?" then you're not really serving that client, and you're certainly not building a viable relationship.

DIFFERENT BUYERS REQUIRE
DIFFERENT APPROACHES

In my experience, there are two types of buyers: (1) The people who want to know what the list price is and then what their discount is, and (2) those who just want to know what the bottom line is and who might say something like, "give me my net price." Recognizing the difference between these clients can help you recognize very quickly how you can best meet their needs. Client relationships are key, and you don't want to sound like customers are viewed only in terms of sales.

Once, when I was calling on a company, the first thing out of the manager's mouth was, "What's my discount?" That was before we'd even discussed the products, much less the price.

I told him, "That depends. If you don't buy anything, your discount is 100 percent—but if you do buy something, it will be less than that." But how I turned him from a bargain hunter into a customer was by asking questions about the company and discovering that they were buying stuff from multiple companies around the globe, when they could much more easily source everything from us. We had domestic stock, we were fast, we were dependable . . . and we were competitive.

Again, the question came, "Well, what's my discount?" At the time, we were selling through some new channels that were not necessarily loyal to us; they were also shopping the globe, so we were losing a lot of opportunities.

So I said, "I could sell it to you for the same price that I'm selling to current distribution—how does that sound?" That piqued his interest. I knew that was a risk, but the channels were few, and the opportunity was tremendous. It was a calculated risk that has paid off. Even those other channels grew with us as we grew in the market.

Recognizing the kind of buyer you're talking to and being able to position the sale appropriately is critically important to how you price your products. That was my first foray with that company, and it took a while to build up trust. There were a lot of players in the market, so there was a lot of history; people had been doing business with the same companies for years. Even though we'd been around for a long time, we were the new kids on the block to that particular industry. This was a growth industry, and although it had been around for a while, the industry was picking up momentum and had started to expand tremendously. When I went to see clients like this, I often spent the whole day at their site, bouncing around from one department to another; the running joke was that I'd be there to open up in the morning and to lock up at night. I didn't realize at the time how important that was, but I was definitely making an impact. Even though it wasn't showing up on my P&L at first, I was gaining rapport, respect, and recognition.

When you look at your customers, recognize their long-term value because that's their true value. If you're crying over the spilled milk of the little details, the opportunity costs, lost costs, or additional loss of margin values on this particular order and you feel taken advantage of, that's the wrong attitude to have. You have to be back tomorrow to win another order, and you'll make it up in the long run—there's no doubt about it. If you're a smart businessperson, you'll find a way to make it up.

It's not about taking advantage; it's about service. It's not every time that your customers are going to ask you for a favor or a better price. If you're competitive, smart, and you do your homework, you'll find that sweet spot. Your customer needs that extra help occasionally, and your ability to give them that help will win you loyalty points. The important things are to maintain flexibility and to take the long view of the relationship.

"CUSTOMER"? MAYBE WE SHOULD USE ANOTHER WORD

Jay Abraham talks about changing your language regarding customers and referring to them as *clients* instead. Customers are transactional—they're just people who buy from you—but clients are people to whom you provide some guidance and advice. You become integral to them and vice versa. That's how you create the long-term relationships we're talking about—the ten-year clients.

People do business with people whom they like and trust. If they like and trust you, they'll be back to do more business. If they don't like and trust you, count your blessings that you have them, because it won't be very long before they find somebody they like and trust better than you.

Shift your customer focus to more of a client focus. If you own a 7-Eleven store, you're going to have both "customers" (passers-by who stop in for a Slurpee) and regular clients (the folks who live down the street and come in every morning for their coffee). Do you treat these people the same way? If you're running a business of any kind, you need to start seeing all of your customers as potential clients and treating them with the consideration required to grow a long-term relationship. World Wide Metric is making that shift, and I can tell you that it's had a significant impact on our clients and the way we do business.

Chapter Five Takeaways:

Read: *Psycho-Pictography* **by Vernon Howard**

1. Define the true value of a client, not just the sales they give you today or this year but over ten years or lifetime. That is a much different number. It will shift your mind-set.
2. People are still the central element of all relationships— don't take any one of them for granted.
3. Approach each client differently and in a personalized way. Listen, ask questions, and learn about them.

CHAPTER SIX:

Your Values Define You— and Your Company

As unique as World Wide Metric is, people could buy and sell via other companies at any time. So why do they choose us? At the end of the day, we're all selling more or less the same products, but customers want to buy from people they like and trust. The things that set us apart from others are our people and the service we provide.

Think about today: This morning, you woke up, brushed your teeth, and took a shower. You got dressed, had your cup of coffee or tea, maybe grabbed some breakfast, and got on with your day, whether that meant the morning commute, opening your laptop, or heading off for an appointment. You and only you had that absolute unique experience that brought you to this very moment in time. Not one of us, even if we were standing right next to each other, had the same day or exactly the same experiences because everything is unique to us. That makes each individual unique because not only did we not have the same experiences today, we also didn't have the same experiences yesterday, the week before, the month before, and so on. That historical chain of events that is uniquely ours—that creates our perspective—is as unique as our DNA. That's an empowering, amazing thing to think about . . . how exceptional each and every one of us is. And no matter what business you're in or what industries you serve, it all comes down to the people within your company. They're the differentiating factor. They are the DNA of your company.

But how do you bring all of these disparate people and their experiences together to pursue the common goal of success as a company? In a word—values. Values apply not just in a general sense but more so as the core that defines how you interact with the world both as a company and as its individual representatives.

DEFINING OUR VALUES

Defining values in a meaningful way that allows buy-in from the people at all levels of your company is a long-term proposition. Respect and loyalty have always been core values here at World Wide Metric, probably reflecting my father's previous career as a ship captain. But putting names to the kinds of values I wanted to see held and reflected in our culture took some time.

We wanted to have a values statement in place, so one day my brother and I went offsite, sat down, and came up with a list of what we thought our values were. We came back the next morning and said, "Everybody, here are our values. This is what we believe in, and so should you."

Everybody kind of nodded their heads and said, "Yeah, that sounds good," but not a whole lot happened after that. Clearly that wasn't how values statements worked.

"Passion" was a word we floated around that didn't quite get to the essence of what we were trying to convey—passion for quality and for service at work but also a passion for outside activities that bring meaning and excitement to life. I still believe that passion is an important component to being a successful employee here because truly passionate people will bring the same excitement to their work as they do to the rest of their lives and be that much more invested in work. But not everyone is fortunate enough to have that kind of engagement, and the word didn't resonate strongly enough to become a value.

In looking for a way to create a meaningful values statement, I decided to try an exercise called "Trip to Mars." In this exercise, you're asked to choose three or four people at the company whom you'd send on a trip to Mars. What skills would they bring that you think would be valuable? How would they serve as ambassadors for the company to the martians they met? And what are the values you'd want them to share? It was an interesting process to go through, and in doing so, we discovered that the phrase that best describes the really successful people in our organization to be "dedicated and driven." They're dedicated in the sense that they're loyal to the company and to customers, they're dedicated to the learning process, and they want to be successful and helpful in many ways. They've got that can-do, will-do attitude. They take initiative. They're enthusiastic. They take ownership. And they're driven by that dedication to deliver the best service experience.

Next, we did a session with the leadership team, and that's when the values were drilled down and clarified. We came up with a list of thirty or so words and phrases that we felt were meaningful values and began to weed through them, eliminating some and finding better words to express others. We talked at length about definitions: What does "continuous learner" mean? What does "driven and dedicated" really mean?

Ultimately, three qualities—continuous learning, driven and dedicated, and being professional—were the ones that rang out to us, the ones that we could hang our hats on and say, "This is the kind of company we want. These are the kind of people who succeed here. This is what we want to hire for, and if people aren't meeting these values, these are the values that we're willing to fire somebody over." In order to understand if something is truly a core value, you have to ask yourself if you'd to be willing to fire somebody over it.

Clearly, this isn't a process that happens in a day. You don't come in and say, "Okay, these are the three values. You guys are good—you stay. You others, you're not up to snuff, so you go." You can't do it like that, because you'd destroy your business overnight. But conceptually, through training and developing and repeating these values over time, you will find people gravitating toward them or going away from them. It's a process, not just a one-time pill.

When we first started with the whole values creation process, we put the values in place, but what did we really do to promote them? What did we do to facilitate them? What did we do to stand by them or stand for them? When we started asking ourselves those kinds of questions, we realized, "Wow, we just learned something new. We've got to do a better job promoting this." We have just begun and still have a lot more to learn.

CONTINUOUS LEARNING

A core value for us is continuous learning. It's my belief that learning is what life is about from day one, and it's a process that should never stop. It's unfortunate that many people, when they grow up or finish with their schooling, never pick up another book, take up a new hobby, or pursue a lifelong interest. Being a lifelong learner and going beyond what you currently are is what life is about. As a business owner, you should live this value and stress it in everything that you do with your people, starting with your training.

Not a day goes by that I don't learn something new. I've been in this business for twenty-eight years now and still get excited as hell when I find something new in a day because it goes to show how much there is to learn. As I tell my kids, "I know just how much I don't know, and that's a lot." If you want to excel and succeed beyond your current calling, you need to learn something new. Lifelong learners are eager to learn, quick to learn, interested, and curious. They are good listeners, they're focused on self-development, and their impetus to learn comes from within. My parents are big believers in lifelong learning, are avid readers, and are constantly curious to learn more about anything that is interesting to them. We have discussions on current events or politics or anything that would be new to us.

Typically, the people we hire are not industry-specific people; we hire from outside of the industry, and we teach them from the ground up. The first thing they have to learn about is the metric system. They may know the difference between Celsius and Fahrenheit or a meter and a yard, but beyond that, most Americans are clueless about metric. The learning process requires some intellectual curiosity and willingness to learn, so it's important for me to be sure that potential hires have those qualities. Those qualities, as it turns out, are common of avid readers, so one of the first questions I ask any potential hire is, "What do you like to read?" or "What have you recently learned?"

Mind you, I hated to read as a kid; I got through high school by writing book reports based on movies. Somehow I got by reading *CliffsNotes*, but I had lost out on a whole realm of learning and understanding. Today, I'm a voracious reader. I was twenty-five years old when I finally fell in love with reading, and I have been addicted to print ever since. I have a personal library that's a good four hundred books deep and continues to expand. There's not a week or a month that goes by that I'm not buying a new book or audio program, because I constantly crave information.

I also believe in rereading; as Darren Hardy says, "Instead of reading ten new books, why not try reading one book ten times?" While I haven't read anything ten times yet, except maybe for this book. I have a list of personal favorites that I return to again and again for inspiration: Napoleon Hill's *Think and Grow Rich*, Dale Carnegie's *How to Win Friends and Influence People*, Jim Collins's *Good to Great*, and a few others. While the books don't change, I do; I've grown and evolved between readings, so my understanding has grown, and I find new nuggets of wisdom to harvest in the rereading. If you have books like that—books that resonated with you in the past and that you haven't revisited—you'll find rereading them from your evolving perspective to be an interesting exercise.

I find ways to encourage my team to look at books as problem solvers, too. If an issue is brought to my attention, along with guiding them through the process of solving the problem, I'll say, "You know, there's a great book on this particular topic that I think would benefit you and give you a whole new understanding. The next time something like this comes up, you'll be much better prepared if you've read it." Then I follow up with them later about what they gleaned from that book. I also buy copies of books I love and pass them around at work. As an employer, if I model a behavior, it will be copied.

DRIVEN AND DEDICATED

We have competitors in the marketplace that do very similar things as we do. But they don't do it exactly like we do. It may look similar, but there are worlds of difference in how we do things, how we react, and how we think.

Years ago, when my dad first started this company, it was built on a simple philosophy. We didn't call it a "value" at the time; we didn't even think of it as a philosophy. It was the "mission," and it was "What can be done today will be done today." That was something we stood behind, and we still do. When customers call us at 4:59 p.m. and ask if we can still ship their order out that day, our team will pull it out of inventory, package it up, and get it there. If we have to run over to UPS and drop it off in person, we do that. We go out of our way to make sure we get the job done today.

> What can be done today will be done today.

There were many afternoons when we would get that last call of the day, take the order, pull the product, and wait until seven or eight in the evening for the trucking line to show up. There were times when they didn't show up, and we would put the box in our car or truck and drive it to the trucking depot. As long as it was there by eight o'clock, it would still go out for delivery on time. This is what

I (and most people) would consider going above and beyond the call of duty. The best part was that our customers didn't even know what we were doing or how we got it done. All they knew is that the order showed up as promised.

We understand our customers' need for speed, and we want to be as fast as we can be at everything we do. The feedback from our customers is great: "You guys get back to us faster than anybody else." I actually get calls from my competition because it's faster to get a quote from us than from their own company! It's not just the systems we have in place; it's the people who make it happen. And that's the critical thing here; we're driven and dedicated to being the best. Each of our branches works together to get the job done because they can't serve the client unless everybody cooperates. We're constantly looking for ways to improve and streamline the customer experience, and a big piece of that is making sure that the different departments are working hand in glove. We support that with team-building exercises for management and supervisors because if you don't do those kinds of things on a regular basis, your people tend to isolate themselves. That creates fractures that can split your company apart.

PROFESSIONALISM

Because we were in a family business, professionalism was one value that we resolved to promote and uphold in every situation. It's not that we were ever unprofessional; it's just that in the internal dynamics of family businesses, sometimes the family part gets in the way of the business part, and the business can lose its professional edge. Those of you already in a family business or who have worked for one know exactly what I mean. The imperative here is to understand that we are family, but we must act professionally. That's why being professional is something we feel very strongly about, and it is one of the core values that we've adopted and work hard to maintain.

What *professionalism* means to us is doing the right thing when no one's watching, having self-respect, having integrity, and having high standards. Be on top of your game in whatever job that you do. Respect those with whom you work as professionals, too, and expect that respect to go both ways. How we think of ourselves and how we treat others dictates how we're seen.

> How we think of ourselves and how we treat others dictates how we're seen. Every day, in everything you do, find a way to get a little bit better.

Another part of being a professional is never being wholly satisfied with how you do what you do. Every day, in everything you do, find a way to get a little bit better. You don't need to make a huge change, but you should strive to make finite, small, incremental changes every day. Over time, that kind of focus can lead to huge changes in you and in your business. These changes can work both ways: if you're making the effort to eat a little better every day and get some exercise, those are positive increments. On the other hand, falling into a daily fast food habit will also have an incremental impact on your health—just not one you're happy about. That's why it's critical to be mindful about making those small, positive adjustments in your desired direction rather than letting the changes make you.

STAY THE COURSE

We all have many distractions, attractions, and shiny stuff around us that can lead us astray from a goal, a vision, or a mission, both in life and in business. Too often, we don't create a big enough beacon to guide us or enough goals to set as our mile markers. If you haven't seen any mile markers for a while, there's a really good chance that you might be on the wrong road, and you need to figure out where you are. Get on the GPS, get yourself back on the right road, and determine that you're moving in the right direction. It's never too late to correct your course. Even planes veer off their designated paths—except at two critical points: takeoff and landing.

I've said this before, but it bears repeating: the best time to plant a tree is twenty years ago. The second-best time to plant a tree is today. No matter what kind of culture you're trying to develop—whether it's a business culture, a family culture, or a personal culture—it's all a choice. You can choose not to pay attention to it. You can choose not to get involved. You can choose not to do a lot of things. But you can't complain about what you get or when you get what you don't want, because you're going to get something, and life has a way of delivering the goods—no matter what. It's a question of what you're asking for. If you don't define your values very specifically, you're going to find yourself not getting what you want or getting what you don't want. As they say in preschool, "You get what you get and don't get upset."

When I was a kid, I wanted to be a rock star. I wanted to play like Eddie Van Halen, and I dedicated hours of time to practicing his song "Eruption." I had a friend who'd just taken up guitar; I played it for him, and he thought it was a really cool piece of music. A month later, he came over to my house, very excited, and told me he'd learned how to play "Eruption." I was still hard at work trying to master the piece, so I said, "Yeah, whatever, sure you did." And then he picked up my guitar and railed away. It wasn't like Eddie played it, but it was a whole lot better than I could play it. I stood there with my mouth hanging open. I said, "How the heck did you do that?"

He said, "I just played it a thousand times a day, and all of a sudden I got faster and faster and faster, and now I can play it." *Poof*—there went my rock star dreams. Somehow I'd thought that it would happen magically. I didn't realize just how much work I was going to have to put into my dream to make it happen or that I might not have the necessary musical gifts.

It wasn't until I grew up that I realized I had another shot at being a rock star—in my industry, in my business. See, most bands that make it to the big time or actors who shoot up to stardom have been in the game for years. They were nobodies, paying their dues and working hard on their craft with little or no success, but all the while, they were honing their skills. It takes time and effort to be recognized as an authority or rock star. It never happens overnight. We may not have quite yet reached rock stardom here, but if our efforts continue and the skills are improving, perhaps one day someone will recognize me and say, "Hey, there's Eddie . . . I mean George." I guess it will depend on whether I am holding a guitar or a valve.

When my wife says to me, "We need more friends," I tell her, "We don't need more friends. We just need to see the friends we have more often." It's the same with customers. We don't need more customers, but rather, we just need to see our customers more often. Right now, we're data mining through years of company history. We're looking for trends. If a customer bought Product A, when are they likely to buy Product B? We are using that statistical information to begin driving processes and procedures in our organization to move it up to the next level. We need to learn more about our customers' needs. And this requires us going deeper in order to become a more integral part of their supply chain so that we can better understand what their current needs are, what their upcoming needs are likely to be, what hasn't worked, and what has worked. We want to know as much about them as we can because we want to help as much as we can.

Values matter, and when you know what you believe and hold valuable, making decisions is easy. The last thing you want is to have multiple ideals and multiple values in place with no consistency. So for our company, we have our three values on which we base our decisions and actions upon: being a continuous learner, being driven and dedicated, and being a professional. What about you? What are the values in your company?

Chapter Six Takeaways:

Read: *Compound Effect* by Darren Hardy and *The Five Dysfunctions of a Team* by Patrick Lencioni

1. You and your company are unique . . . embrace that fact.
2. Your values help define that uniqueness.
3. Go back and read a book you have already read. The book hasn't changed, but likely you have. Over time you should have a few great books that you have read up to ten times. (See the appendix for a list of my book recommendations.)

CHAPTER SEVEN:

B Positive—It's Not Just a Blood Type

Positivity is not solely dependent on the events that you experience. Rather, it is how you think about those events and choose to react that matters. Is your way of thinking helping or holding you back?

Life and business are full of choices. When you wake up in the morning, you can choose to jump out of bed and be excited about the day, or you can roll out of bed and moan, "Oh, jeez, another day." Sometimes it's hard to be clear that this is, in fact, a choice. What motivates this choice? Is it coming from a place of being positive, or is it coming from a place of being negative? Is it coming from a place of being proactive, or is it coming from a place of being reactive? Are you responding reactively to something? Is negativity your knee-jerk, go-to response? As the leader, whatever attitude you bring to work will affect everyone else's attitude. It flows from the top down.

As an example, picture my sales team coming to me and complaining about an ongoing issue. They want me to fix it, but they also recognize that it's something that might not be fixable. I could say, "Well, sorry guys, you didn't make it. Better luck next time," but that's not necessarily a useful reaction. A better, more constructive approach is to listen and to ask questions that lead them to consider the ways we could turn the situation into a positive one. A better approach would be to say, "Let's take a look at what happened. What did we miss? What could we have done better?" I could certainly be the answer person, but if I give them the fish, they only eat for today. If I teach them how to fish, they will be able to eat for a lifetime.

When my team leaves my office, they're better prepared to deal with a similar situation down the line in a more positive, constructive way. A constructive thought process may go something like, "Last time we didn't make it. These were all the reasons. This time, instead of waiting until June 2 to come and talk to you about why we didn't make our month in May, we're coming to you daily, saying, 'Hey. This is what our expectation is. How do we get these things locked and loaded so we can earn our commissions?'" That's the kind of proactive, positive mentality that I want my people to embrace and move forward with.

People have a strong tendency to want to throw whatever bad stuff is coming at them onto your desk to deal with and walk away, an action that essentially says, "Here, you need to fix this." I think that letting that happen is a big mistake. As leaders, we tend to have the knee-jerk response of, "Oh yeah, leave that with me. I'll take care of it." So now the monkey is off their back and on yours. Bad choice.

What ends up happening is that you collect ten or twenty "I'll-take-care-of-its," and all of a sudden you're overwhelmed. That's when the negativity starts kicking in, and you are coming down on yourself because you allowed this to happen.

How you look at the world determines how you influence those around you because, as leaders, people are watching us and waiting to see our next move. Now, there are some people out there who think that everybody's out to make sure they screw up and that no one wants to see them be successful. That might be true in some circles, and if those are the circles of friends that you have, you might want to get new friends. But no matter what's around you, you still need to maintain a positive demeanor because you don't know whom you're going to affect. You don't know who is going to be calling you next. You don't know who is going to walk in your door next and what issues they might have. As the leader, if you are caught in a downward vortex of negativity, you're just going to spawn more of the same.

Happy staff equals happy customers. If you're aggravating your staff, chances are they're going to offend your customers. Then your customers come back at you, fighting mad. Then you go piss off your staff, and you've created a nasty little cycle of negativity. Alternately, you have the opportunity to be a positive influence on other people, and I think that people don't recognize just how much of an effect they can have. There is a great line from the Patrick Swayze movie *Road House*, in which he is the head bouncer at a rough bar where the owner is trying to reduce and eliminate the bad clientele. In a meeting with his team, Swayze's character tells them to be nice: if someone is out of line, be nice; if someone is yelling, be nice; ask them again to calm down, and be nice. Show them to the door, and be nice. Continue being nice "until it's time to not be nice."

Don't think that because you're just one person, you can't make an impact. Imagine what the world would be like if Bill Gates or

Mother Theresa had thought that way. You have your own spheres of influence, starting with your family, your friends, the people you know and come in contact with, your staff, your customers, and your vendors. When you start growing that circle little by little, you realize that you actually touch a lot of people.

In the interaction with my salespeople that I described earlier, I could have changed the whole outcome of the conversation depending on how I acted. I could've sent them out of my office, cursing and moaning. Or I could have sent them out feeling optimistic about working toward a solution and seeing the challenge as a learning opportunity that could benefit the whole company. You as a leader need to find ways to present a positive face. Find the silver lining, and send your people back out with that attitude—because that attitude is what your people will take with them to their next client call or phone conversation.

Part of being the leader is accepting the challenges that all the different personalities we deal with bring to the table—and to our offices. You can't plan for everything or for every interaction. What you can plan for is to focus on your attitude and how you come across to others because that will often make a bigger impact than your words.

Much like the saying, "you are what you eat," comes the idea that "you are what you think." Thoughts are food for the mind and emotions. One of my favorite authors, Vernon Howard, points out the fact that the self-talk in

> The self-talk in our minds plays a critical factor in creating self-fulfilling prophecies.

our minds plays a critical factor in creating self-fulfilling prophecies. So if you wake up with a negative mind-set, you're going to go out there and basically look for things to fulfill that mind-set you have. You may think things like, *It's raining today. I hate it when it rains. Now my shoes are wet. My clothes are all wet, and oh, my hair, a bad hair day, and oh, it's raining in my coffee now.* These thoughts can ruin your day—and the day of others—if you allow them to. But if you have a different outlook on your day and think something like, *It's raining today. Great. I don't have to wash my car,* then the self-fulfilling prophecy turns into a positive one. It's not what happened, but rather, it's how you react to what happened and what you think about it.

Now, I'm not here to say that there's a secret formula for being positive every day. The secret formula is in the doing and in the awareness. Awareness is the first thing. The next part is conditioning yourself to try to consistently think like that and to put things in front of you that remind you to hold a positive mental attitude and proactive approach.

For myself, I want to be present. I want to be positive, and I want to be passionate. When I think of my interactions with other people, I want to be engaged.

> Perfect practice makes perfect.

I want to be caring, and I want to be honest. These are things I think about—ideas I hold in my mind every day. In short, I practice it mindfully, which is very important to internalizing it. Mindfulness is defined as a mental state of consciousness that is achieved by focusing one's awareness in the present moment. They say, "Practice makes perfect." That's not really true, but practice does make permanent. If you keep practicing the wrong thing, you're going to make that a permanent bad skill. So change that to perfect practice makes perfect. Being mindful is a constantly active effort.

Consider golf; let's say you have a bad slice. You go to the range and slice hit after hit. When you're done, what have you really accomplished? You have practiced a bad slice over and over again. That's not the right way. Get a lesson or two, straighten your drive, and *then* practice that over and over so that perfect practice makes permanent. But when it comes to work, there's little or no time to improve and practice a skill before you actually implement it with customers.

A lot of what we do in business is learning by doing. You go on a sales call with a customer, and if you're not prepared, either you're going to throw up all over their shoes or they're going to show you the door. And you're going to say, "Oh, that went terribly," figure out what you did wrong, and go back and do it again properly. There's not necessarily anyone saying, "Hey, let's go and practice a couple scenarios here ahead of time." That seems crazy to me, especially if you compare your preparation time to how athletes typically prepare for games. Professional athletes spend 90 percent of their time practicing and less than 10 percent of their time actually playing.

The business world doesn't work that way. In the business world you work five days a week, and then there's the weekend mentality of, "Okay. Recover, drink heavily, and come back to work on Monday. But don't worry about practice." Elite athletes get paid a lot more than most businesspeople, and if you wonder why that is, take a look at how much you're practicing compared to how much they're practicing. They make an art and a life out of practice. That's their job— to practice. The game is just the end result of what their practice gave them the ability to do.

In an earlier chapter, I talked about Michael Jordan and his extraordinary accomplishments. He had a relentless training regimen, and he practiced longer and harder than just about anybody on his team. He had an extraordinary work ethic. People point to him and Tiger Woods as examples of highly gifted athletes, and that's undeniable—but what sets them both apart is their relentless work ethic in building on their innate gifts. I think that's what it takes, and I also think that most people, unfortunately, just don't want to work that hard. But if you knew that you could raise your game to the level of a Jordan or a Woods, wouldn't you put forth the effort? Even today, Tiger is trying to regain his greatness with a new swing, a new coach, and a whole lot of practice. The jury is still out on whether his regimen will pay off and if he will once again regain his greatness. Nothing is guaranteed in life, but with hard work and practice, you too will see improvement and positive results with the right attitude.

A lot of people will think about rising to the level of Jordan and say, "Well yeah, but that's just not going to happen." Next year will be here sometime in the next 365 days, and whether we like it or not, the clock is ticking. The question is, are you going to do something today toward achieving what you want, or are you going to let time slide? Will that New Year see you closer to a goal, or will you find yourself sliding back and making excuses?

For myself, I think that everything is possible. All you need to do is put forth the right attitude, have that mental focus, and start doing it. Go plant some trees. It's never too late.

My father has been a powerful influence in my life, even though I didn't always listen very well. I heard, but I didn't actually listen, and when I say "listen," I mean that I didn't act. My father used to always tell me, "Learn from other people's experiences," and I'd always say, "Well, secondhand experience is still secondhand. I need to experience it for myself." I was fortunate that he let me make my own mistakes. Unfortunately, it took me a lot longer to get through the learning curve of life than it should have because I was stubborn, and I thought I knew what I wanted. My father had a tough life. He had no father as he grew up, and he had to fight to make his life into the success that it is. I know now that a lot of what I perceived as negativity from him was really just a reflection of his past experience. Part of my own maturation process, and perhaps the most important part in terms of my world view, has been being able to take what I believe he meant, what I see now as his desire to help me grow up right, and actually reframe the memories to a point where whatever I perceived as being negative is now a positive thing in my mind. When I do this, I catch myself sounding just like my dad, which is usually a really great thing.

When I worked at Dale Carnegie, there was an exercise we would do at meetings: you pick one person and go around the room, and everybody has to say something nice about that person. At one point it was my turn, and my colleague Linda turned around and said, "You know George, the one thing I admire most about you is that I know that you don't have a good day every day. I know that sometimes you feel like crap. But every single time I say, 'How are you doing, George?' you always tell me, 'I'm great.' I know you're not, but you always say that you are, and I love that about you because you're always positive."

No matter who you are, everyone has problems in life. The last thing people want to hear you do is whine and moan about yours. But I find that people with problems come to me because they need that ray of sunshine that I'm going to shine on them, saying, "Hey. Listen. It's not all that bad. Let's find something good here. Let's look on the positive side." I'm not here to fix people, and I've recognized that (although when I was younger, I thought that I was). But I can see that my attitude is catching, and if I can help someone get past a bad place and to a better one, that's good for everyone and for morale in general.

IF YOU WANT MORE, YOU HAVE TO BECOME MORE

Author Jim Rohn says that if you want to be more successful, that doesn't mean you have to put in longer hours and harder work. What you really need to focus on is getting better at what you do; if you want more, you have to become more. If you want more money, you don't just go out and work ten more hours. What you need to do, as Steven Covey would say, is to "sharpen the saw, like the lumberjack."

Here's the old story: A lumberjack came to a logging company and asked for a job, saying, "I'm the best logger around." The boss told him they weren't hiring, so the lumberjack offered, "Let me go down and cut some trees, and if you think I do a good job, then you pay me," and the boss agreed.

So the first day, he goes out there and cuts down five trees. He comes in and marks it on the board that he cut down five trees, and the boss says, "Oh, very interesting. Come back tomorrow, and we'll see how you do." So the lumberjack comes back the next day, but he only cuts down four trees because he's so tired from the work he'd done the previous day. He sees the other loggers sharpening their saws and thinks, "What a waste of time; I'll beat these guys easily tomorrow." The third day, he gets there extra early, but he can only manage three trees. The fourth day, he comes in super early and he stays extra late, and he actually gets up to four trees again.

The boss takes him aside. "You're a little bit erratic with your production. What's going on with you? You're all over the place."

The lumberjack says, "I don't know. I worked really hard the first day. I thought I worked just as hard the next day, but it was less productive. The third day, it got even worse."

The owner says, "Let me ask you a question—how often do you sharpen your saw?" and the logger couldn't remember the last time he'd done that. So he sharpened his saw, went out, and cut down five trees that day—and he did it more easily than he'd cut down three the day before.

Want to sharpen your saw? Check your mental attitude toward the world around you because that's going to affect your productivity and your interactions with other people. It all starts with having the right attitude on the inside, which makes it much easier to get through the day—just like a sharp saw cuts faster through a tree.

Chapter Seven Takeaways:

Read: *The 7 Habits of Highly Effective People* **by Stephen Covey and** *Psycho-Pictography* **by Vernon Howard**

1. Everything begins and ends with your attitude. You must learn to be mindful of this in all you do.

2. Grab an index card. Write down three descriptive words that you want to mindfully focus on. For me these are: present, positive, and passionate. Now write down three descriptive words that you want to mindfully focus on in your interactions with others. For me these are: engaged, caring, and honest.

3. You cannot be all things to all people, so don't be. But you *can* be mindfully focused.

CHAPTER EIGHT:

Respect and Trust Start with You

*"He will win whose army is animated with the
same spirit throughout all its ranks."*

—*Sun Tzu,* The Art of War

I talked in an earlier chapter about the tendency we have as entrepreneurs to think that somehow we can or should be able to do it all and the trouble we often have with delegating jobs to others. What does that really boil down to, in simple terms? I suggest that it speaks to a basic lack of respect and trust.

It's surprising how close those two words are in definition. One is a feeling of admiration for someone or something that is good, valuable, or important. The other is a belief that someone or something is reliable, good, honest, and effective. The first one is the definition of *respect*, the second the definition of *trust*, and to me it's hard to see which is the chicken and which the egg.

RESPECT GROWS DIVIDENDS

A big mistake that entrepreneurs and second-generation leaders make in running a company is missing the opportunity to build trust and to respect people in a way that pushes them to grow because by growing your people's abilities, they're going to do a better job of serving the customer.

I think that the process of becoming a good leader starts with healthy self-respect because that allows you to give respect to others and earn the respect that they'll give you back. Some people go at it with the idea that because they're the boss, they're automatically entitled to respect. But without giving respect and trust first, you're playing a losing game.

I'd go so far as to suggest that a lot of start-ups that go broke in the first year or two do so because of the leader's lack of trust and respect. It might not be the business model, it might not be the pricing model, it might not be the customer base, it might not be the industry, and it might not be the economy; at the core, it's all about the people.

The flip side is that leaders who are effective are invariably those who treat others with respect and trust *first* because you're only going to be lifted as high as your team will lift you. You must delegate, trust, and respect your employees and give them the opportunity to rise and prove themselves—ultimately, that's how you rise and how your company succeeds.

> You're only going to be lifted as high as your team will lift you.

My dad was a captain, but to achieve that he had to work his way up through the ranks and earn the respect and the trust of those above him and around him. Keeping a crew of one hundred working as a unit is a tough assignment; you have all the challenges of running a ship and the power of the sea on all sides to test you. It takes a major team effort to pull that off and to literally keep your head above water. You can imagine the level of trust—in both directions—that captaincy entailed and how everyone's survival depended on his ability to lead. Respect was the number-one value in my house.

WHY IS THE PROBLEM ALWAYS THE YOUNGER GENERATION?

Every generation seems to say it of the next, upcoming generation: "Kids today have no respect." Generation X is looking down at generation Y, saying, "Look at how they are acting like idiots," and everybody else is saying, "These Millennials are the worst." I know that boomers' parents thought the same of them: "Those crazy hippies."

What are we doing when we say stuff like that? We're disrespecting that younger generation, calling them out on things that, once upon a time, we were probably called out on. Maybe it's just the natural progression of life and that people end up putting other people through what they went through because that's the rite of passage of a generation. But when you think about it, it's not right to generalize about a whole generation and say, "They're all like that," when that's not true. I've met many millennials who don't give a damn about social media. And not every baby boomer smoked marijuana. Shocking, I know!

When you look at something like lack of respect in the workplace, one of the most damaging forms of colleagues disrespecting each other is backbiting—the water-cooler gossip. People are so quick to throw others under the bus and create little tribes around themselves. It's like high school, with the nasty little cliques. People will shun someone they perceive as not pulling their weight and push the weak one out like a runty puppy. It's our job as leaders to recognize those dynamics and deal with them. Very often, you find that shunned people have the attitude they do because they've been disrespected for their whole lives, and because of their low self-esteem, they're willing to take it on the chin. And that's a shame because they end up succumbing to self-fulfilling prophecies, and they won't allow themselves to aspire to be more.

So by taking that lone wolf under your wing and offering them some respect and trust, all of a sudden they open up like a beautiful flower. They begin to thrive just because someone cared enough to trust them, gave them a little respect, gave them some dignity, and stood by them when no one else would.

The fact is that we all want trust, respect, and dignity. We all crave them. We all need them. But most of us don't give out those things enough, because we see it as a "you first" hierarchy. We're under the assumption that, "Oh, they have to respect me first because I'm older," or "They have to respect me because I'm the boss," or for any of a number of reasons. Ask people what they did to earn respect, and chances are all they can offer is that sense of entitlement. That's not good enough.

Respect and trust are things that you earn every single day—whether it's with your clients or your staff or anybody else in your life. They don't come on a silver platter; they don't come in a birthday box; they don't come packaged any which way. Respect and trust are things that you have to actually work at. One blind spot that people commonly have is that they don't recognize that they actually have to *do* something to earn trust and respect, and that like anything and everything worth doing in life, it takes an effort.

IT'S ABOUT CHARACTER

People think that golf is hitting a ball and chasing it up and down the fairway to put it in the little hole. And although that *is* what we do, that's not what golf is about as a social exercise. When you're out there playing with a colleague, a customer, or a vendor, the one thing that everybody looks at is how you behave. Are you getting pissed off every time you make a mistake? Are you cursing or throwing your club? When you go to the restaurant, are you treating the staff there like servants? "Go fetch me a drink, hurry up. What took you so long?" Or if the waiter spills something on you by accident, are you telling him or her, "You have to give me a free dinner," or "I need money to pay for the dry cleaning bill"? How someone treats people at that level tells you a lot about his or her character.

When we're hiring people, I look at attitude and character. Do they talk about their previous bosses in a respectful manner, or are they quick to throw them under the bus? It doesn't mean that the boss wasn't a jerk and every bit as bad as this person's saying, but it does show me that this person has no respect for that boss. Everyone can get one really bad boss in a career, but if you're telling me negative stories about three or four, I'm going to wonder if you have an issue with authority or respect, not to mention question if you're trustworthy. If you don't give respect, my assumption will be that you didn't earn any either. If someone with those kinds of attitudes does get into the organization, be quick to get him or her out because those attitudes can spread like cancer.

WANT TO BE A GOOD PERSON? BE WITH GOOD PEOPLE

I try to align myself with like-minded individuals, with people who have a good attitude and good character and who treat everyone they meet with respect—even if those people don't necessarily show themselves to be worthy of that respect. Period. Any other kind of attitude is just unacceptable to me.

This requirement can be challenging when it comes to raising kids, but it's very important; when I was young, my father was very tough on my brother, my sister, and me, to the extent that it often challenged my self-respect. As I grew up and realized that he was pushing me to be my very best, I appreciated his efforts now more than ever, even if his methods were a little rough. I have learned that I can make a positive difference if I show respect before expecting it, and you'll see the people around you blossom with that kind of treatment and rise to meet your trust. On the flip side of that, I am certain that there are a lot of people who would have benefited, as my siblings and I did, from tough love. As a matter of fact, I believe that more kids today would benefit from tougher love. There is too much softness in our language and actions, especially with children; we don't want to upset them. We don't want them to be on the losing team, so everyone gets a trophy. Hogwash. What happens to those young adults when they enter the real world and life smacks them upside the face? They will not be ready for what the world is capable of dishing out. My dad prepared us to deal with the toughest minds, the loudest voices, and the biggest egos—all while being humble. It really has been a unique experience and not one that is easily replicated. We are fortunate. I just hope some of that will rub off on my kids as well.

As a leader, you have to understand what your responsibility is as the role model. When I talk about being a professional (one of our values), it's about doing the right thing when no one is watching, having integrity, and having high standards. You have to be honest and trustworthy. Being a professional in my world also means being respectful of yourself and of other people. All those good things will come back to you if you are those things first.

I read a great story once in a book called *The Art of Possibility*, written by a gentleman named Benjamin Zander, a conductor for the Boston Philharmonic, and Rosamund Stone Zander, a psychotherapist. The story was about a school teacher who, on the first day of class, told his students, "You all have an A in my class. Now, it's your job from this day forward to keep that A. And here is what you have to do to keep that A: you have to come to class, you have to do the assignments, and you have to do well on the exams." By the end of the year, that class had more 'A' grades than any other—and not because the teacher was giving them out but because the students were rising to meet the level of respect he'd offered them. This is a great story to think about when you look at working with people because we all crave respect; even though we may not say it, we do. When you're giving respect upfront, as a leader, you're setting the expectations, and the majority of people will strive to live up to them.

PRAISE PUBLICLY, REPRIMAND PRIVATELY

This is a big one and a common mistake that otherwise smart leaders sometimes make. Who hasn't heard the horror stories about a boss berating an employee in front of his or her peers? That the person getting berated loses respect for the boss; the staff watching that person getting berated also loses respect for that boss because they feel sorry for the person he or she was berating. Even if what that employee had done was really bad, the sting of public humiliation comes across as worse.

But do praise in public because boosting people up also boosts you up. If you have to give someone bad news, do it privately. There is no sense in shaming someone in front of everybody, and there is nothing to gain from it.

DO HOLD PEOPLE ACCOUNTABLE

The risk with the "speak softly" strategy is that to some people, you will seem insufficiently tough. If you're not holding people accountable, you'll generate ill will: "Why the hell are they keeping this loafer around here? They should terminate this person." And the longer you take, the faster the respect that they once had for you diminishes. You have to understand that as a business owner or a leader, respect is all around you, and perception rules. If your people perceive that you're

> You have to understand that as a business owner or a leader, respect is all around you, and perception rules.

being weak, or if they perceive that you're being brutal, they're going to lose respect for you. And that's the worst thing that can happen because when you need your staff most and when the company needs to be strong, if the leader is not being respected, the trust is not going to be there—and neither will the business, eventually.

I don't need people to love me, and I certainly don't need anybody to fear me, because as long as they respect me, that will get the job done much better than either of the other two could.

ARE YOU CONTAGIOUS?

I mean "contagious" in the sense that to drive the business, to get to the level that you want to get to as a business leader, you need to be a passionate, enthusiastic, flag-waving cheerleader for your company. I think that when you look at sales and marketing, you find that their roots are in respect and enthusiasm because selling and marketing is a contagious thing. When people get excited and enthusiastic, it breeds more of the same and draws people who will want to do business with you. As a leader, earning the trust of your staff, your customers, and your vendors starts with respect, and it's ultimately the leader's responsibility to start that ball rolling. I have a lot of energy and enthusiasm; it's just integral to who I am. Not all leaders are naturally outgoing or enthusiastic. Maybe you come out of finance, and your style is more "head down" and analytical. But you can still broadcast respect for others in a quieter way by how you react, how you listen, and how you ask questions in a discussion. When people feel heard, they feel respected.

Respect is like a bank account. When you open a bank account, you put the first deposit in, and then you add to it over time. If you put in more than you take out, you start building a balance. If at some point you have to make a withdrawal or if you made a mistake along the way, you have a cushion to fall back on while you work to rebuild that precious asset.

Chapter Eight Takeaways:

Read: *The Art of Possibility* **by Rosamund Stone Zander and Benjamin Zander**

1. Respect is like an investment. You have to give it first before you get any return.
2. Surround yourself with people who demonstrate the qualities you most admire.

CHAPTER NINE:

Let Your Reach Exceed Your Grasp

In an earlier chapter, I talked about the efficacy of setting business goals in an orderly, meaningful way. But my addiction to goal setting is as much personal as it is professional, and I'm just as rigorous about writing down those personal goals. You should be, too.

Years ago, I started to write my goals on a three-by-five card that I would slip in my wallet, right next to my money. Initially I would read my goals literally every day—sometimes several times a day—until they were committed to memory. Every time I go to pull out my credit card, every time I go to pull a dollar out of my wallet, I always touch that little three-by-five card.

I've heard it suggested that you should write a goal down, put it in an envelope, put the envelope in a drawer, and then open and read it years later. Let's say that you want to sell your company five years from now—what's your magic number? Write that number down, and throw it in the drawer. Don't look at it until the day someone wants to buy your company, and then see if that number is the same number you're getting. That's a great exercise, but it doesn't deal with the kind of goals I'm talking about here. I'm talking about the real, tangible things that you want to achieve. Putting them on a three-by-five card and putting that in your wallet is a very important first step.

When writing down your goals, don't forget to include the reason *why that goal is important to you.* Just like in the cash flow model discussed in an earlier

> "When you have a big enough reason *why,* the *how* is easy."

chapter, cash is oxygen to a business, and the "why" is the oxygen to goals. A goal lives and breathes and can be achieved because there's a big reason behind it. It's been said that, "When you have a big enough reason *why,* the *how* is easy." As an example, let's say that you have a general goal to lose weight. Then, all of a sudden, you find out that you're prediabetic and diabetes is in your future, which means that now your life is likely going to be shorter and much less healthy. But if you choose to focus on losing weight, you might be able to preempt diabetes and live a healthier, longer life. How much more powerful is that as a *why?* And how much more heft does it bring to an otherwise nebulous goal?

This is exactly what happened to my cousin. He was 285 pounds, and he was prediabetic. His father had died from diabetes. Whether he liked it or not, he was on the verge of it. My cousin decided at some point that he'd had enough. I had given him a book *Diet Evolution* by Dr. Gundry, which is about healthy eating habits, and before long, he went from 285 pounds down to 170 pounds. He's no longer on that path to ill health and an early exit. What made it possible? For him, he had a big enough reason why. He had a wife and a new child, so it wasn't just about being at a healthy weight. It was about living for his family. What are your reasons why?

ARE YOUR GOALS REALLY YOURS?

As important as it is to nail down goals, it's equally important that they be the right ones for you. If you can't come up with a compelling reason why a goal is important to you, chances are that it's not really your goal—and it might be somebody else's. Far too many times, those of us with parents who have aspirations for us, whatever they might be, have had those goals imposed on our lives for so long that we begin to confuse them with our own hopes and dreams. We may dedicate our lives to fulfilling those goals—even though they aren't really even ours—because we've internalized them to such a degree. And often our lives will be miserable because of that. Check to make sure that your *why* really holds water and is a driving force for you to achieve.

IS ACHIEVING YOUR GOAL GOING TO MAKE YOU HAPPY?

We assume that it will, of course—but unfortunately, for far too many people, that's not the case. It's no different in business. You think that becoming an entrepreneur and a business owner is what you really want, only to find out that you've just become your own employee—except that you can't take a day off. You can't take a vacation. You have to pay everyone else first, and you don't even have enough money to pay yourself. The stories go on and on about these kinds of unhappy outcomes for business owners, especially entrepreneurs and small business owners.

I contend that a big reason that so many start-ups fail is because they were started with the wrong goal. You open a business thinking, *If I open this business, I'll be happy. I'll have everything I'll ever want.* But the fact of the matter is that you probably haven't identified everything you ever wanted, and those things you identified as real wants probably weren't your wants in the first place. It often takes time to recognize our real goals. It's a mindfulness exercise that's worth doing right because doing it wrong can leave you frustrated and stuck in a place where you don't want to be.

Look at your *why*, and ask yourself, "Is it compelling? Is it big enough? Is it really something that I can sink my teeth into?" If you can answer those questions positively, then go for it. There shouldn't be a reason not to do that. But if you find yourself scratching your head and saying, "Well, it's what my parents wanted for me," that's certainly not a compelling *why*. It may have seemed to be one, but do you really own it?

MY GOALS—LANGUAGE

I'm not a wordsmith by any means. But I have come to understand the art of communication, and communicating with other people is one of the most important skills anyone can have, particularly if you're running a business. Word choice is a big piece of that skill. I tend to drop F-bombs quite often, although having kids has made me work to curb that habit. But the bigger goal in improving my use of language is to eliminate those moments when I'm thinking, *What's the right way to put this? What's that word?* because not having mastery of the vocabulary you need is an impediment to good communication.

Another piece of the communication goal is knowing how to best communicate to the audience to which you are speaking because you have to tailor your language to the person you're speaking to. And when I'm around someone who has a prolific grasp of the language and is throwing words at me that send me to the dictionary, I love that opportunity to learn. I mentioned earlier that lifelong, continuous learning is a value for both my company and for me, and I find that there's always a word out there I've never heard but really need to know. I used to keep a dictionary on my desk, and I would joke with people, "Any time you feel that by the end of the day, you haven't learned something new, come into my office; we'll crack open the dictionary and find a word that we both can learn today. We'll make sure we both at least walk out with one or two new words, even if we haven't learned anything else."

James Robbins wrote a book called *Nine Minutes on Monday*, and it's a great management tool. He talks about the use of language and how we talk to ourselves and to other people. I found one story in the book to be especially meaningful: Two friends are meeting for lunch one day, one of who had recently survived cancer. At some point, the recently recovered friend inquired, "So what are you going to do for the rest of the day?" His healthy friend replied, "Well, I've got to go meet my wife, and we've got to go over to my mother-in-law's house, and we've got to go do this and that and the other"—a laundry list of all the "gotta-dos." Then he asked, "How about you?" And his friend answered, "Well, I *get* to go with my wife to my mother-in-law's house, and we *get* to have dinner together, and then we *get* to go to the movies and hang out together." With that one word, he made the clear distinction between obligation and privilege.

I love that story because it underlines for me how deeply our language can both reflect and influence our thinking and how we view the world.

GOAL SETTING IS A LONG-TERM PROCESS

This is not a seven-minute abs workout. This is life workout. When people asked Michelangelo, "What do you see when you look at a piece of stone?" he would tell them that he didn't see the stone—he saw the piece of sculpture that was hidden in it. All he had to do was chisel off the pieces that didn't belong there. That's how goal setting works. It's about seeing life differently. It's about *doing* life differently. It's about thinking about life in a more positive, productive manner. It's looking at life in the big picture, at the long-term scheme of things, even though your time could be up tomorrow. The only moment you have is the moment of now. They call it the present for a reason: it is a gift. You can't change yesterday, and even the greatest planner can't guarantee that tomorrow will come for him or her. Now is the time to start setting goals because too often, people wait for the optimal moment—the optimal time, when the weather's just right, when the wind is blowing at just the right speed—when everything's in perfect alignment. "When I get to that final, perfect body weight, then I'll take my shirt off and go to the beach." What if that moment never comes? Would you regret never having put your feet into the sand and sea just because of some condition you invented that you had to meet first? People who live their lives like that find themselves unhappy. They find themselves unfulfilled. They find themselves not achieving—being stagnant.

THE TRAP OF LIMITING BELIEFS

Limiting beliefs can come from within us or from outside influences. Very often we inherit them from our parents and from their language. Words have power, and words sculpt our view of the world and our place in it. They define what we believe we can accomplish and what we think we can't do.

When you hear people talk, you can hear their limiting beliefs and where those limiting beliefs lie. If you take the time to read up on neurolinguistic programming (NLP), you can see how the use of language can affect many things, and it can help you take back the power that you may have ceded to someone else or to limiting beliefs—wherever they've come from. I know this worked for me; I believe it can work for you. It's power, and it's freedom.

HOW DO YOU BEGIN?

The best way to start is . . . to start. What I like to do is to start with a blank sheet of paper and just begin writing.

Try it. Write anything and everything that comes to your mind, and list as many goals as you can that pop up. If money didn't matter, if time didn't matter, if everything and anything was possible, if the world and the stars in the universe would line up to support you, and you could have anything if you put your mind to it, what would you wish for? Start there, and make a big list. Eventually you'll have to whittle these goals down, but this is a great way to start.

BHAGs are one of my favorite things to write about because they're what dreams are made of. I guarantee that anyone who has made a tremendous success of himself or herself, whether you're talking about Sir Richard Branson or Bill Gates, had a BHAG in their mind at one point in time or another, and they've brought that to fruition in their lives because they put it out there. If you don't put the BHAG out there, if you don't have a Big Hairy Audacious Goal, don't expect Big Hairy Audacious results.

Now, that being said, if your goal is to become a billionaire by Saturday—well, you might need to be a little more realistic. If you're just out of college, don't have a dime in your pocket, and don't come from a wealthy family, then the likelihood of you becoming a billionaire by Saturday is nil. You have to start with some sense of reality as to where you are in life. When you start there, you can start working outward, ticking off one step at a time.

When I have my own big laundry list of goals down on that paper, I start to go through them. Which of them could I realistically accomplish in the course of six months? What might take a year to get done? The first step to accomplishing them is to put a time frame on each of them, whether it's a twenty-four-hour goal or a lifetime goal that I'm going to put in the ten- to twenty-five-year bucket because there's a whole subset of goals that have to happen before that big one happens.

When you start identifying the time frame for each of the goals, you can start to identify which ones are subsets of another, longer-term goal. You start to identify incremental steps rather than goals in and of themselves. Begin with the end in mind, and work backward to today.

At that point it's useful to grab another sheet of paper, put that big, long-term, lifetime goal at the top, and start organizing the smaller goals that would fall under that bigger one. Once you've done that, you can start to build out the timeline of achievements toward the conquest of the biggest goal, if that's what you really want to accomplish.

NOW COMES MY FAVORITE PART

Once you get that kind of focus going, that's when you break out the three-by-five card and write down, "This year, here's what I'd like to accomplish." You're now just looking at what's doable in a year, but this is also part of the process of achieving that ultimate goal. Include some smaller steps that you might have to take incrementally, month by month. Also include some activities that you need to establish as daily habits to get there, and don't forget to include your *why*.

Then stick it in your wallet, and read it every day. After you've written a goal, you should review it every day for the first thirty days—as many times as you possibly can reach into your wallet and look at that little card. Where do you find the time for that? Well, there's this place called the bathroom where most of us spend some quality minutes every day, and it's an ideal location for this goal-review activity. You're alone (or should be), it's quiet, and there's not much that you can do other than what you're already doing. Use the time, and make it count toward moving you forward.

ACTION TIME

Now that you've identified your goals and gotten to know them, what comes next? In a word, action. Begin to do whatever it takes to fulfill your goals. It's one thing to write it down and to kick-start this whole process, but nothing happens until you do something about it. Once you establish a goal, the very first thing you have to do is take massive action toward that goal and its achievement, as Tony Robbins states all the time. And that is just doing whatever that first thing is. If you're fat, and you need to lose weight, that first thing is getting up off your ass and going for a walk around the block rather than to the refrigerator. That simple act is more effective and more profound to the overarching scope of a goal than anything else (with the exception of the *why*). It's that action you take by getting up and taking that walk. It's the action you take by picking up the phone and calling that customer who you desperately want to do business with but have been too meek to approach. It's the action of you calling them; it doesn't matter whether they say yes or no. The point is that you took the first step. You took the action. It's about walking up to that girl or guy and complimenting her or him—making that first effort that could turn into a lifelong relationship. Don't be afraid; *be bold.*

And guess what? Once you start acting in that manner, and you repeat that action over and over again, then before you know it, those cumulative actions are going to add up to a result. And the result is either going to benefit you or change your mind, and then you can reevaluate it and make adjustments accordingly.

DON'T BE AFRAID TO COURSE-CORRECT

Establishing a goal doesn't mean that it can't change or that you can't decide to change it. You might realize that, "I thought I had a good enough reason, but that just doesn't make sense anymore." That's okay. As long as you're okay with it, it's okay. It all comes down to the simple choice: you have the choice to do it or not to do it.

Those are the biggest things that I've learned when it comes to goal setting. You simply have to put yourself out there and take steps toward the goal. If you don't take steps toward it, God doesn't come down and open the doorway for you—although I do believe that once you start taking action, if you are on the right path and have a big enough *why* attached to your goal, there is a higher power that will shine light on you and help you along the way. The universe has a way of getting in alignment with you when you're in alignment with your goals. Sometimes it teaches you lessons and diverts you, and you need to be willing to divert. You're supposed to learn a lesson along the way.

It takes action. You can't just wait for the door to open. You still have to turn the handle and walk through, and sometimes there's a long hallway to walk down before you get to the other side. But the point is, the door's unlocked—what's required of you is the action.

Make your first action grabbing that sheet of paper and making your own list. Start now because you are planting the seed that will take you to a bigger, better future.

Chapter Nine Takeaways:

Read: *The Compound Effect* and *The Entrepreneur Roller Coaster* **by Darren Hardy**

1. Write your goals on a three-by-five card and put it in your wallet next to your money.
2. Make sure each goal has a reason why associated to it. The bigger the why, the more likely it will be achieved.
3. Read the card often and continually focus on the key steps to achieving your goals.

IN CLOSING. . .

I wish someone had told me a lot of the things in this book a long time ago because I'd be a lot closer to my personal goals than I am now. But like they say, you eat an elephant just one bite at time.

My parents helped lay the keel and the foundational values of my life. They have been there guiding me every step of the way, and I am here because of them. I've also been lucky enough to fall in with some pretty smart people who have helped me to formulate and get clear on many of my own goals. I suggest that you spend the time cultivating relationships with some people who are like-minded when it comes to personal and business growth because you'll learn more by listening than you will by talking. One great place to meet people like that is in mastermind groups.

Napoleon Hill talks about mastermind groups in *Think and Grow Rich*. A mastermind group is a group of individuals who have similar interests or ideals but who may hold very divergent opinions and come together to share them. To get that kind of input, we joined a group called The Alternative Board (TAB). World Wide Metric has our internal board of directors, which is basically our family. Family businesses can get somewhat insular in their thinking and approach, though, so I think it's critical to look for fresh ideas outside of your industry and certainly outside of your own company.

Because TAB's board was made up of leaders from different business backgrounds, it gave me insight into various different industries. They all ran very different types of companies, from insurance to software development to manufacturing. But despite the diversity in what we do and how we do it, certain things remain the same for all of us: we all have to deal with people—whether you are talking about communications, employee relations, customers, or management—and people are people, no matter where you find them. TAB is a great place for all of us. It is an opportunity to talk openly about challenges we face, to listen and offer advice, and just to let our hair down, peer to peer. Most of us are far more frank in there than we'd be with our respective boards of directors or staff. Among peers there are no preconceived ideas; there was no downside to being open, because whatever we discuss is confidential. It allows us the breathing room we all need to function.

For me, this mastermind group is probably one of the most useful and fruitful things I do because again, "you can't do all, and you can't do it all alone." Everyone needs some sort of assistance, guidance, mentorship, and idea sharing. Years ago I wrote a mission statement that started off with the idea that I want to surround myself with positive and like-minded individuals who sought for personal excellence within themselves. For the most part, I am an upbeat, energetic person, and I tend to gravitate toward positive-minded, optimistic people. When I come across pessimists or people who are down on life and down on their luck, my first inclination is to want to help them. But many people don't want the help; they're happier in their misery, and nothing I could say or do could ever change that about them. And even pessimists can bring something important to the discussion because they have their own points of view, and some of them are realistic and useful.

Don't fear opposing points of view, because you need a balance. There's the Yin and Yang of life. You cannot have the optimist without the pessimist. You can't have the positive without the negative. You cannot have the good without the bad. It's just that I chose to be on one side more than the other.

Some people love Tony Robbins—I think he's great, and his enthusiasm and optimism speak powerfully to me. Some people find him too rah-rah. I believe a lot in what he says, and as I learn more about him, I've come closer to the sources of the knowledge that he brings to his work; I read the guys that he read to get to where he is. I have come to learn and understand how much I don't know. That's why as a leader, I am more inclined to keep my mouth shut, to see what other people know, and to see how much they understand because maybe I could learn something. I'm perpetually in that mode. I think it's imperative as a leader that you be humble and check your ego at the door because no matter how hard you work, it's a life of perpetual learning, and you will never, ever learn it all or learn enough. And when you have an opportunity to mentor and teach someone, take that opportunity because it's a two-way street. When you teach something to someone else, you learn it that much better.

For me, this writing process is not so much about sharing my knowledge or teaching other people as it is a personal, therapeutic process of relearning and reteaching myself all the things that I already believe and know to try to be a better version of myself. This whole life is about learning and improving, about trying to be the best you can be whether you're a dad or mom, a son or daughter, a business owner, a manager, a supervisor, a sanitation worker, a truck driver, a clerk at Walmart, or a McDonald's fry cook or a rock star. Whatever you are in life, be the best "you" you can be.

Do the best job that you can because there's no reason not to. It takes just as much effort to do a good job as it does to not do a good job. It takes as much effort to be lazy as it does to get off your ass and do something. Find the next steps toward the next steps and keep moving. You can't stop. Complacency is death. Stagnation is death.

Take the leap of faith, and take the step toward that thing that you aspire to be and that you want to become. As Jim Rohn says, "Work harder on yourself than you do on your job." When you affect others, when you bring *you* to the office, when you bring *you* to the game, when you bring *you* to the meeting, you'll be delivering "You 2.0"— and that will make all the difference. Live life—don't let life live you!

My Top 100 Recommended Reading

Title	Author
1. Getting Everything You Can Get Out of All You've Got	Abraham
2. The CEO Who Sees Around the Corner	Abraham
3. The Sticky Point Solution	Abraham
4. Driving Excellence	Aesch
5. 2 Seconds Lean	Akers
6. Getting Things Done	Allen
7. Illusions	Bach
8. Selling the Invisible	Beckwith
9. Execution	Bossidy
10. The Charge	Bruchard
11. First Break All the Rules	Buckingham
12. Now Discover Your Strength	Buckingham

13.	The one thing you need to know	Buckingham
14.	How to Win Friends and Influence People	Carnegie
15.	The Leadership Pipeline	Charan
16.	Influence	Cialdini
17.	Good to Great	Collins
18.	Great by Choice	Conley
19.	Peak	Connors
20.	Oz Principle	Connors
21.	7 Habits of Highly Effective People	Covey
22.	Keys to the Vault	Cunningham
23.	ROAR	Daum
24.	Tilt	Dawar
25.	Oh, the Places You'll Go	Dr. Seuss
26.	Managing for Results	Drucker
27.	The Effective Executive	Drucker
28.	The Power of Habit	Duhigg
29.	Simplify Everything	Epner
30.	Go for No	Fenton
31.	Never eat alone	Ferrazzi
32.	The World is Flat	Friedman
33.	The Checklist Manifesto	Gawande
34.	The e-Myth Revisited	Gerber
35.	The Sales Bible	Gitomer

59.	The Art of the Advantage	Krippendorff
60.	The Five Dysfunctions of a Team	Lencioni
61.	Guerrilla Marketing	Levinson
62.	Buy.ology	Lindstrom
63.	Make the Noise go away	Linne
64.	The Power of Full Engagement	Loehr
65.	Fish	Lundin
66.	Dig Your Well Before You're Thirsty	Mackey
67.	The Greatest Salesman in the World	Mandino
68.	Turn Your Ship Around	Marquet
69.	Changing the Channel	Masterson
70.	The 5 levels of leadership	Maxwell
71.	Crossing the Chasm	Moore
72.	Hard Goals	Murphy
73.	Lead the Field	Nightengale
74.	Crucial Conversations	Patterson
75.	The Power of Positive Thinking	Peale
76.	In Search of Excellence	Peters/ Waterman
77.	Drive	Pink
78.	The Think Big Manifesto	Port
79.	Spinselling	Rackham
80.	The Ultimate Question	Reichheld